I0462365

*The Ultimate Fundraising Guide to*

# GETTING PAST
# THE GATEKEEPER

Inside Secrets, Simple Tips and Proven
Strategies for Getting Your Foot in the Door
with the Most Hard-to-Reach Major Donors,
CEO's, Celebrities and Political Big Shots

## Dr. Chuck Muth, PsD
*Professor of Psephology (Homeschooled)*

No portion of this publication may be reprinted or reproduced in any way without the author's express written permission. A reproduction of even a single page is a violation of United States and international copyright law. Violators of this agreement will be prosecuted to the fullest extent of the law.

We're not kidding.

Copyright © 2014 by Chuck Muth and Desert Fox Strategic Communications, LLC.
All rights reserved.

Desert Fox Strategic Communications, LLC expressly disclaims all warranties as to the contents of this publication including, without limitation, the implied warranties of merchantability, fitness for a particular purpose, infringement, and makes no warrant as to the results that may be achieved by using this information contained in this publication. Because this information can be used in a variety of ways to fit various purposes, Desert Fox Strategic Communications, LLC will not be responsible for any damages (including, without limitation, indirect, consequential, special or punitive damages) suffered or incurred by any person arising out of such person's use of or reliance on this publication.

Reproduction or translation of any part of this work without permission of the copyright owner is unlawful. Requests for permission or further information should be addressed to Desert Fox Strategic Communications, LLC.

# DEDICATION

This book is dedicated to six individuals who most influenced its creation.

To Gary Halbert, rest in peace. I met Gary sometime around 1992 at a conference at Bally's Hotel in Las Vegas. That meeting set me on the path of direct response marketing and a lifetime of continuing marketing education.

To Brad and Alan Antin, two direct response marketing geniuses who I met at the same conference with Halbert and whose strategies and tips for getting past the gatekeeper were the inspiration for this book.

To James Malinchak, the *Big Money Speaker*, who inspired me to just get the book done without worrying about the cover not looking perfect. As James is wont to say, *"My ugly book is better than the one you ain't got."*

To Henry Evans, my business coach, mastermind leader and author of *The Hour a Day Entrepreneur*. Henry's book-writing workshop gave me all the information and tools needed to finalize and actually publish this book.

And lastly, to my assistant Midori Grino, without whom this book might never have gotten out of my computer and into print.

Thank you, all!

# CONTENTS

# INTRODUCTION

My name is Chuck Muth and I'm known as *The Campaign Doctor*™. Yes, I've given myself that name and title – which is driving some in the medical profession absolutely bonkers!

I'm the son of a Baltimore City firefighter and stay-at-home mom. My dad went to night-school to get his college degree... then served four years in the Maryland House of Delegates. And my kid brother once worked for a U.S. congressman.

So politics runs in the family.

I'm also the president of a non-profit grassroots lobbying organization called Citizen Outreach - which in 2003 I took from zero to over $1 million in revenue less than 18 months later!

Oh, and I've been blogging since long before the term *blogging* was even invented. *Muth's Truths* is the #1 conservative political/public policy blog in Nevada. And *Citizen Outreach's Nevada News & Views* newsblog is the #1 portal for other conservative bloggers, commentators, columnists and citizen journalists in the state.

Over the years I've been published, featured or quoted in national publications such as the Wall Street Journal, USA Today, Roll Call, the Washington Times, the Washington Post, The Hill, Politico, the Daily Caller, TownHall.com, National Review and U.S. News & World Report.

I've also appeared on major network affiliates as well, including ABC, NBC, CBS, FOX, CNN, BBC and even Al Jazeera America. Plus countless numbers of talk-radio programs.

But believe you me… I'm anything but an *overnight success*.

I actually got my start in politics way back in 1992 when I joined the local Republican Party central committee in Las Vegas.

Three years later – despite not even knowing what Robert's Rules of Order were, let alone how to follow them! - I managed to be at the right place at the right time and accidentally got myself elected chairman!

But I knew my limitations.

So I raised the money I needed to enroll in the Republican National Committee's Campaign Management College in Washington, DC which was, at the time, being run by Newt Gingrich and his top political strategist, Joe Gaylord.

CMC was an intense weeklong school starting at breakfast and running well into every evening.

We're talking 7:30 a.m. until 10:00 p.m. - plus homework!

We were taught by some of the best in the business back then, including: Barry Hutchinson, Terry Cooper, Dave Winston, Bill McInturff, Bill Greener, Dan Hazelwood, Shelly Kamins, Mary

Heitman, Jack St. Martin and Evelyn McPhail.

We learned messaging, opposition research, issue development, targeting, polling, campaign management, photo ops, PACs, events, voter ID, media, communications, voter contact mail, television & radio advertising, coalition development, get-out-the-vote, list development, volunteers, scheduling, campaign strategy, and perhaps most importantly…

BIG money fundraising: Major Donors, Finance Committees, Events and Direct Mail.

All topped off on the final day with a series of political *war games*.

And by the time I left Washington and flew back to Nevada, I knew exactly what I wanted to do: Help other conservative candidates, campaign managers & party leaders also learn how to REALLY run a WINNING campaign.

But it's one thing to learn about running a campaign from a textbook or training manual; it's another thing altogether to learn from actually doing it.

So a couple weeks after returning home, I agreed to run for the state Senate against the Democrat Minority Leader in a district with a 3-1 Democrat voter registration advantage.

Now, I knew from Day One that I didn't have a prayer unless my opponent got indicted or died (neither of which happened). But for me, the motivation wasn't so much to win as to get the practical experience that would give me the *moral authority* to stand before a bunch of inexperienced candidates and teach them what they should be doing.

Indeed, I know where you are... because I've been there, done that!

To make a long story short, as expected, I lost in November.

Immediately after, however, I began traveling around Nevada doing campaign training seminars for local candidates and party activists based on what I'd learned at the Campaign Management College.

Eventually I began traveling around the country doing training seminars for the Republican National Committee, GOPAC and the Leadership Institute, as well as many on my own.

Over the years I've literally trained thousands of candidates on campaign fundraising, campaign strategy, campaign communications and campaign management.

"Getting Past the Gatekeeper" is an extension of my live training seminars, making this invaluable information available to countless numbers of candidates, activists, party leaders, campaign managers, and, really, every and any person involved in some kind of sales – political or otherwise.

One last thing: While acknowledging that getting past the gatekeeper is often the most difficult challenge, I've included two bonus chapters at the end of the book which gives you additional tips, tricks of the trade and strategies for what to do and say AFTER you've gotten past the gatekeeper.

The real key to your success, however, will be whether or not you actually use this information and implement it. Regrettably, many readers won't. Don't be one of them!

Now let's begin...

# TESTIMONIALS

*What People are Saying About the Campaign Doctor*

"Dr. Muth, I am a fan! Without your information I start feeling a little isolated and wondering if there are new ways to 'get more donors' that I'm missing for my clients. Thanks for the tips and insights."

**Sally A. Nungesser**
*Nungesser Consulting LLC, Baton Rouge, LA*

"Chuck, I do indeed enjoy all your campaign stuff. While the good Senator has been at this for a long time, it is always good to get some fresh tips!"

**Barbara Grassley**
*Wife of Iowa U.S. Sen. Chuck Grassley*

"Hi Chuck. The Fed Ex man just rang my doorbell. He brought me a very impressive package with the FAST Start Fundraising guide and workbook inside. I started reading the moment I opened it and I can't put it down! What a gold mine of invaluable campaign information. I just wish I would have had this 5 months ago when I decided to run!! Many thanks."

**Jill Dickman**
*Reno, Nevada*

"Having worked in campaigns for many years, I still get something new from every workshop you put on that I attend. Thank you for keeping your seminars current and fresh."

**Ralph McMullen**
*Former Chairman of Washoe County Republican Party*

"I attended my first Campaign Doctor seminar last week and was so impressed with the amount of knowledge that was shared. The ideas went from simple to 'Wow, why hasn't anyone else said this!' You really get what a sales and marketing job running for office is (I'm not sure many understand this concept at all!). It was hands down the best training I've attended."

**Amy Groves**
*Las Vegas, NV*

"Your workshops are simple, direct, to the point, and would make a candidate following your advice a force to be reckoned with."

**Bill Thornhill**
*Las Vegas, NV*

"I wanted to see what your introductory 3-hour political training seminar was about but my wife had extremely high negative interest, so I had to promise we would find a way to sneak out if it was boring. To say the least, the seminar was anything but boring.

My wife was riveted by the presentation, quality and totality of information given. Even though I have considerable political experience, I took 8 pages of notes in 3 hours. The motivational aspect of the seminar was a huge unexpected bonus."

**Eric Burgess**
*Chicago, IL*

"One word about the campaign hot tips newsletter: FUN. When I open it my immediate reaction is a smile. This isn't some painful thing to read/learn. I wish I had school books like this when I was in school. I would have paid attention."

**Jim Bieber**
*Bieber Communications, Southern California*

"I've known Chuck Muth for over a decade. He has always given great insight and advice on what it takes to be a good candidate. The Campaign Doctor is an appropriate title for Chuck. He can identify what ails your campaign and he will always give you the right prescription to fix the problem."

**Gary Bernstein**
*Executive Producer, HoodworX Entertainment*

"It is Psephology Today, Campaign Doctor and Winner's Circle that helped get me to where I am today. I took notes on your campaign guides and kept them on my desk. I turned your advice into actions. I listened to your CDs in my car instead of the radio.

As a first time candidate, I found your Campaign Hot Tips exceptionally helpful. The one thing that I had the least of in my campaign, was time. Your hot tips were full of information and a fast read. They took up very little of my time. And the best part is, the tips WORK!"

**Phil Regeski**

"You packed in 8 hours worth of value in a 3 hour evening. The '20 Questions' for candidates alone were worth the price of admission. I knew that vetting questions were needed, but yours are concise, to the point, and require realistic reflection."

**Jeff Waufle**
*Las Vegas, N.V.*

"I was at your workshop last night in Reno. Wow! I had no idea how much I didn't know about running for office! It was the best money I've ever spent, and one of the most entertaining 3 hours and 15 minutes I've ever enjoyed.

It is the rare individual who can make a three hour training session both inspirational and fun. You are certainly that rare individual."

**Jeffrey Purtee**
*Reno, Nevada*

"The thing I liked best about your seminar was the use of humor, anecdotes, and the handouts. If you are a beginner, like me, running for office, I strongly suggest you make an appointment with the Campaign Doctor. You will be amazed how much you don't know about organizing, financing, and winning a race for public office."

**Jim Bathgate**
*Carson City, NV*

"I found Chuck's seminar to be very informative and helpful. After two unsuccessful campaigns, I plan to implement his ideas and suggestions when I run again. I now feel optimistic that the odds of my success have greatly improved."

**Scott Chappell**
*Las Vegas*

"I can't imagine trying to run a political campaign without the key people going through Chuck Muth's campaign workshop. It was a fast-paced combination of best practices, discussion, and must-have takeaways needed to win."

**Lynn Muzzy**
*Minden, NV*

"Are you running just to run or are you running to win? If you're running to win, Chuck Muth's workshop is a campaign curriculum prerequisite."

**Jason Woodbury**
*Carson City, Nevada*

"Chuck Muth's campaign seminar was fabulous. I am running for office and I found all the information to be invaluable. It is a must-take seminar if you are running for office or if you will be one of the support people for a candidate."

**Barbara Altman**
*Las Vegas*

"I attended Chuck Muth's enlightening and entertaining workshop last night. Chuck is a neat guy who has been teaching all phases of campaigning for over fifteen years.

Although I have a strong background in communications and classroom teaching, I picked up a number of valuable tips and ideas. No, I'm not a shill!"

**Jerry Smith**
*Reno, Nevada*

"Politics is a tough game and Chuck Muth's insightful approach shows you how to use fastballs, curves and sliders to win your election. He's entertaining and spot on!"

**Larry Walsh**
*Gardnerville, NV*

"Every candidate should attend this workshop – if they are interested in winning."

**Todd Taxpayer**
*Reno, Nevada*

"I have taken a number of Chuck Muth's campaign classes and have learned more than I could have ever thought I would. As a candidate, I cannot express how important it is to take these classes."

**Vicky Maltman**
*Sun Valley, NV*

"The workshop was very informative and helped me see a different side of politics. With these helpful tips in mind I hope to try my hand at campaigning sometime soon. Thanks a lot!"

**Victoria Brunson**
*Las Vegas, Nevada*

"I found Chuck's seminar to be very informative and helpful. I would highly recommend it to anyone running for office."

**Lisa Krasner**
*Reno, Nevada*

"Regardless if you are a seasoned politician or a first-time candidate, an experienced political operative or a novice wanting to wade into the political arena, everybody young and old will benefit significantly from the training seminars that Chuck Muth has to offer."

**Jerry Stacy**
*Reno, Nevada*

"What stood out was your presentation, which comes from a place of passion and concern. It is clear to anyone that you are the junkie's junkie when it comes to politics and elections. Anyone would be an idiot to ignore the good and proper advice and direction that you provide."

**Glenn Sherman**
*Las Vegas, Nevada*

# THE FOX AND THE GEKKO

In fundraising – which is nothing more than a form of sales – the fact is it often takes as much time and effort to get a $25 donation as it does to get a $1,000 donation.

So why not shoot for the grand, right?

And when it comes to fundraising events, adding a *celebrity* appearance to the invitation is almost guaranteed to boost interest and attendance…the bigger the name, the better.

Ditto fundraising letters and even endorsements.

Problem is, how does a little guy like you…especially if you're an unknown, wet-behind-the-ears novice candidate…get an audience with *Mr. Money Bags* for a big donation or land *Mr. Big Shot* as a speaker at your event?

Here's how…

Do you remember the original 1987 *Wall Street* movie starring Michael Douglas and Charlie Sheen?

In it, Sheen plays Bud Fox, a small-time stockbroker who wants to make it big by landing big-time Wall Street mogul Gordon Gekko as a client.

Fox spends the first part of the movie just trying to get a one-on-one personal meeting with Gekko. Indeed, the hardest part turns out not to be getting Gekko as a client…but just getting the appointment!

Fox finally gets his foot in the door by showing up at Gekko's office on Gekko's birthday.

> *SIDE NOTE: Which reminds me: If you have any kind of customer/client/donor database whatsoever, the most important piece of information you should endeavor to find, in addition to basic contact info, is the person's birthday. Once you have that, all kinds of cool things are possible. More on that later…*

Long story short: Fox gets his meeting with Gekko, makes his pitch and shortly after returning to his office gets a call from Gekko giving him his shot at the brass ring.

Hanging up the phone, Fox exclaims, incredulously, *"I bagged the elephant!"*

> *The Lesson: Before you can bag the elephant, you have to make your pitch. And before you can make your pitch, you have to get an appointment.*

The Big Kahunas aren't Big Kahunas for nothing. They're extremely busy and are usually guarded by extremely efficient screening systems and *gate-keepers* designed to keep riff-raff like you from wasting their time.

So yes, the hardest part is often just getting your foot in the door...which is what you'll become an expert at by the time you finish reading this book!

# THE RULE OF COMMITMENT

By the way, when most people think of the phrase *foot in the door*, they probably conjure up an image of a door-to-door vacuum cleaner or encyclopedia salesman inconspicuously sticking his foot in the door once an unsuspecting housewife makes the mistake of opening it.

At that point, the woman is unable to close the door and end the sales pitch until the salesman is finished making his presentation.

In modern day sales, getting one's foot in the door has more nuanced meaning, especially when it comes to fundraising. Here's how Wikipedia explains the technique at it relates to charitable donations:

> *"There are a number of studies concerning the foot-in-the door technique and charitable donations. For example, Schwarzwald, Bizman, and Raz (1983) investigated the effectiveness of the foot-in-the-door technique for door-to-door fundraising.*

> *"In their study, some of the participants were first asked to sign a petition before being asked to make a donation to the organization (foot-in-the-door condition). Others were not asked to sign a petition before making a donation (control condition).*

*The request to sign a petition was made two weeks prior to the request to make a donation.*

*"They found that a greater percentage of people made a donation in the foot-in-the-door condition than in the control condition. Also, they found that making the small request to sign a petition resulted in more money being donated than not making this request."*

In campaigns and for many grassroots organizations, you see this technique used all the time on the Internet. Folks are asked to sign an online petition urging, for example, Congress to vote for or against a certain bill.

*That costs the person nothing.*

But once they've made this first little step – a commitment - the campaign or organization has their *foot in the door* and can follow up with a request for a donation from someone who has already raised their hand and said, *"I'm interested."*

The power of this technique, which preys on the deep-seated human desire to be consistent, is further demonstrated by a 1960s experiment by psychologists Jonathan Freedman and Scott Frasier, as explained by Prof. Robert Cialdini in his excellent book, *Influence: The Psychology of Persuasion*:

*"A researcher, posing as a volunteer worker, had gone door to door in a residential California neighborhood making a preposterous request of homeowners. The homeowners were asked to allow a public-service billboard to be installed on their front lawns.*

*"To get an idea of just how the sign would look, they were*

*shown a photograph depicting an attractive house, the view of which was almost completely obscured by a very large, poorly lettered sign reading DRIVE CAREFULLY.*

*"Although the request was normally and understandably refused by the great majority (83 percent) of the other residents in the area, this particular group of people reacted quite favorably. A full 76 percent of them offered the use of their front yards.*

*"The prime reason for their startling compliance has to do with something that had happened to them about two weeks earlier: A different volunteer worker had come to their doors and asked them to accept and display a little three-inch square sign that read BE A SAFE DRIVER.*

*"It was such a trifling request that nearly all of them had agreed to it. But the effects of that request were enormous. Because they had innocently complied with a trivial safe driving request a couple of weeks before, these homeowner became remarkably willing to comply with another such request that was massive in size.*

*"Freedman and Fraser didn't stop there. They tried a slightly different procedure on another sample of homeowners. These people first received a request to sign a petition that favored 'keeping California beautiful.' Of course, nearly everyone signed, since state beauty, like efficiency in government or sound prenatal care, is one of those issues almost no one is against.*

*"After waiting about two weeks, Freedman and Fraser sent a new 'volunteer worker' to these same homes to ask the residents to allow the big DRIVE CAREFULLY sign to be erected on their lawns.*

*"In some ways, their response was the most astounding of any of the homeowners in the study. Approximately half of these people consented to the installation of the DRIVE CAREFULLY billboard, even though the small commitment they had made weeks earlier was not to driver safety but to an entirely different public-service topic, state beautification.*

*"At first, even Freedman and Fraser were bewildered by their findings. Why should the little act of signing a petition supporting state beautification cause people to be so willing to perform a different and much larger favor?*

*"After considering and discarding other explanations, Freedman and Fraser came upon one that offered a solution to the puzzle: Signing the beautification petition changed the view these people had of themselves. The saw themselves as public-spirited citizens who acted on their civic principles.*

*"When, two weeks later, they were asked to perform another public service by displaying the DRIVE CAREFULLY sign, they complied in order to be consistent with their newly formed self-images."*

So you can see how having someone who is completely disinterested in your political campaign or organization can be *hooked* into a much bigger role by something as simple as signing an innocuous petition that has absolutely nothing whatsoever to do with your campaign or organization.

But what's that have to do with getting your foot in the door of Mr. Big, right?

Right. Don't worry, I'm getting to that…

# THE RULE OF RECIPROCITY

Also in Prof. Cialdini's book, he explains the Rule of Reciprocity...

*"A few years ago, a university professor tried a little experiment. He sent Christmas cards to a sample of perfect strangers. Although he expected some reaction, the response he received was amazing – holiday cards addressed to him came pouring back from the people who had never met nor heard of him. They received his holiday greeting card, click, and whirr, they automatically sent one in return.*

*"While small in scope, this study nicely shows the action of one of the most potent of the weapons of influence around us – the rule for reciprocation. The rule says that we should try to repay, in kind, what another person has provided us.*

*"If a woman does us a favor, we should do her one in return; if a man sends us a birthday present, we should remember his birthday with a gift of our own; if a couple invites us to a party, we should be sure to invite them to one of ours.*

*"By virtue of the reciprocity rule, then, we are* obligated *to the future repayment of favors, gifts, invitations, and the like. ...*

> *Because there is general distaste (in society) for those who take*
> *and make no effort to give in return, we will often go to great*
> *lengths to avoid being considered one of their number.*

Cialdini goes on to note just how powerful this Rule of Reciprocity is by citing the success the Hare Krishnas have had in getting people to make a contribution who first have a flower pressed into their hands or pinned on their jacket.

This is also part of the reason you see so many businesses offering free samples of their products or services. And why many charitable organizations, such as the VFW, send you those *free* return address stickers along with their donation request letters.

You see, the hardest part is getting someone to try something new for the first time. But after breaking the ice, the rules of Commitment and Reciprocity kick in, making it far more likely to get bigger involvements, sales and donations...or even just a simple appointment.

Let's say you want to make a phone presentation to a potential major donor or corporate executive but have been unable to make first contact and/or have been blocked by a *gatekeeper*.

Try this...

# THE COFFEE BREAK

I learned this one from The Antin Brothers way back in 1992... and the ability to pull it off today is even easier and less expensive than it was two decades ago.

Seems the brothers were having difficulty getting an audience with a certain *editor-in-chief of a major international magazine* who they wanted to promote their new marketing book. After running into several brick walls, here's what they did...

> We went out and got a custom coffee mug printed with a picture of the cover of our book on two sides, and a hand-written message in the middle. The message said:
>
> *"Don't forget: Coffee with Brad Antin, Tuesday, December 22, 1992 at 10:30 am."*
>
> We then bought a very nice silver teaspoon with gold accents, a beautiful black linen napkin, and a special sampler of gourmet coffees that can be brewed right in the cup.

Then we wrote the following little note and stuck it in the cup:

*Dear George,*

> *As hectic as your schedule has been lately, you certainly deserve a break.*

> *Won't you be my guest for a special cup of coffee?*

> *I'll join you by phone on Tuesday, December 22, 1992 at 10:30 a.m.*

*Warmly,*

*Brad Antin*

*P.S. I've already entered the time into my appointment book, and would appreciate it if you would also. Of course, if this time is not convenient for you, please have your secretary call me to reschedule.*

We then had it nicely gift-wrapped in gold foil paper and had it delivered via special courier.

Nice, huh? It works.

# SPECIAL DELIVERY

One quick note here about a reference made in Brad's P.S. from the letter.

I can't remember where I read it – maybe it was something by Dan Kennedy or Gary Halbert – but the point was this: *nobody has ever refused to open a letter delivered by FedEx.*

Again, your message or invitation is a complete waste of time and money if the recipient never opens the letter or package. And while FedEx is certainly more expensive to use than the post office, if you're trying to get in front of a *Mr. Big*, it could well be worth the extra expense.

But if you really want to make an impression…

Use a private courier service.

If your target lives in any city or town in the U.S. with lawyers, you'll likely be able to find a private courier service. Attorneys use them extensively to hand-deliver important legal papers, especially documents that require a signature from the recipient himself, not just his secretary.

Your best bet might be to get a referral from your own lawyer as to who he uses for local courier services, but short of that, just type in *private courier service* and the name of your city or town in Google, Bing, Yahoo or any other search engine and you should pull up multiple options.

If your intended recipient lives out in the boonies somewhere, you'll still be able to find someone to deliver your package…but be prepared to pay a premium for the service.

Also, beware of and ask about additional fees that may be associated with private courier service that some firms can conveniently *forget* to tell you about upfront, such as fuel surcharges, extra fees for late-hour or weekend deliveries, additional fees for delivering to a residential address, insurance, etc.

Now if for some reason you need to have something delivered to someone overseas – an option growing larger every day as the world continues to get smaller thanks to technology - you're going to need an international courier service.

And while I haven't used the following service and, therefore, can't vouch for them, I'll share part of their *About Us* information from the firm's website (*www.privatecourierservice.com*), if for no other reason than to give you an idea of the sorts of things you should look for in a courier service.

> **Private Courier Service** *is a company specializing in hand held, personal delivery of private documents or packages that must be accompanied by a secure and trusted individual worldwide.*
>
> *We will pick up and deliver your items anywhere in the world.*

*Need something delivered to the middle of the Amazon rain forest? Call us. Need something delivered to a war zone securely? Call us. Need something delivered to an office in the middle of Moscow? Call us.*

*We specialize in delivering your documents or package to your recipient anywhere in the world and we do it by hand, securely, safe and confidential! We physically get on a plane, train, boat, car, bicycle, snow mobile or whatever it takes to get your item to your recipient!*

*This is not Fed-Ex, UPS or some other "put it on an airplane and hope it gets there" service. We carry your documents or package on our person and hand deliver to your recipient.*

*Our private courier service is not for everyone. It's for the person or business that needs absolute guarantee of a safe and secure delivery by a reliable and trusted person.*

*There is pretty much nothing that we cannot transport for you. We DO NOT carry illegal items. We won't fly to Sierra Leone, pick up your blood diamonds and deliver them to your broker in the diamond district of Antwerp.*

*That being said if you have legal documents or a package that needs to be delivered in person, privately and confidentially, we will go to all lengths and overcome all obstacles to get it to your recipient!*

The firm is owned and operated by man named Peter M. Humleker Jr., *a United States Marine Corps veteran and experienced world traveler* who, at the time of this writing, lives in Miami, Florida. His phone number is (305) 600-5121 and his email address is *peterhumleker@gmail.com*

Again, I haven't personally used Mr. Humleker's service, but I did call and speak to him prior to publishing this report to confirm the business and contact info. Just do your due diligence before contracting with *Private Courier Service* or any other vendor of any other service for any other reason.

> *Bonus Tip: Have your courier deliver nothing but one of those disposable cell phones. He should text you the minute he gets into the office and in front of "Mr. Big." You call the cell phone. The courier then hands the ringing cell phone to Mr. Big and says, "It's for you."*

You then have Mr. Big on the line!

## CELEBRITY WORSHIP

Having your campaign or organization associated with someone considered to be a Hollywood-type celebrity usually has an extremely positive impact.

We're a country raised on celebrity worship. Think *Academy Awards. People* magazine. *Entertainment Tonight.*

That's why you see so many products and so many services advertised on TV and radio featuring celebrity endorsements.

Now this is truly the very definition of irony.

The main reason you – as an unknown candidate, organization or product – might want a celebrity endorsement, is to give you more credibility in the minds of those who may have never heard of you...which often results in more sales or donations.

So you're boosting your own credibility by being associated with or endorsed by people who make a living pretending to be somebody else! Is this a great country, or what?

In addition, as late marketing guru Gary Halbert explained, when you use celebrities in your advertising you also "get the 'reflected glory' of all their credits because you can *legitimately* mention in your copy all the magazines and the TV shows and movies and stuff they've been in. *More credentialing!*"

And don't think they have to have an A-lister, such as Bratt Pitt or Jennifer Aniston, for you to benefit from celebrity association. Character actors with far less name ID can be great. You just have to do a little education about where they've appeared that makes them a celebrity.

In fact, celebrities appearing on today's *reality* shows – which are all over cable television – are perfectly acceptable. Indeed, almost any contestant from *American Idol, Dancing with the Stars* or *The X Factor* will do as well as some of those old *washed up* actors who appeared on *The Love Boat* and *Fantasy Island* (ask your parents).

And don't think you have to pay and arm and a leg. A dirty little secret in Hollywood is that most actors and actresses are just like the average *working stiff*...often going month-to-month just trying to make the rent.

However...

If you try to negotiate directly with the actor's agent, you're likely going to get nowhere. As Halbert noted in one of his books, the agent "will quote you a fee so outlandish you'll think you asked him the price of a studio, not of a star. And you'll say forget the whole thing and the star will never know the conversation took place."

Instead, Halbert advises, if you submit a specific offer IN WRITING, "the agent is compelled by the ethics of his profession to pass that offer on to his client."

And then it will be up to the actor or actress as to whether or not to take the gig.

Now, that's if what you're looking for is someone to endorse a commercial product or service. To get an celebrity to endorse a political candidate or headline a political event is another animal altogether.

First, most celebrities don't want to get into any kind of political issue or campaign at all, regardless of their own political persuasion. Because once they take a position on a campaign or public policy issue, they risk alienating a significant chunk of their fan base that disagrees.

Secondly, as we all know, there are far fewer conservatives and Republicans in Hollywood than liberals and Democrats. So *slim pickens* isn't just an actor's name.

But if, like Bud Fox, you persevere and don't give up…success *can* be had.

The first step is to identify the conservatives and/or Republicans who have made their political/philosophical leanings publicly known. And this isn't as hard as you might think.

> *"I realize that the majority of people in the entertainment business happen to be Democrats," Beverly Hills 90210 star Shannen Doherty once said. "I have no problem with that. And they should have no problem with the fact that I'm a Republican."*

But they do. And that's why many conservative and Republican celebrities remain, unlike Doherty, *in the closet.* But the ones who are *out* can be found with simple Google searches.

Try searching *celebrity Republicans, celebrity conservatives* and *celebrity libertarians* and you should get plenty of leads.

But again, don't focus solely on A-list names. You'll have far better success if you start small. The celebrity doesn't have to be Clint Eastwood or Bo Derek.

And they don't have to be a Hollywood star. They could be a sports figure. Or a musician.

And they can be a local celebrity, not necessarily a national figure. If they're well known in the district or state where you're running, they might very well fulfill the *celebrity* requirement.

And keep your eyes and ears open to news reports about conservative campaigns and issues which reference individuals who aren't candidates themselves. If they're mentioned or referenced in the news, especially if they're already well known – and they're on your side of the aisle – you might be able to land them.

Of course, once you've identified an individual who fits the category of *celebrity* and appears to be on your side, you have to get an invitation of some sort in their hand. And as you can imagine, it's not always easy to find contact information for a celebrity, especially Hollywood stars.

But it's not impossible.

Sometimes you can just Google a person's name and you'll find they have a website which includes contact information. Sometimes you'll actually find a direct phone number or email address.

In other cases, you might be able to reach them through their Twitter or Facebook account.

In addition, if they're an actor or actress of some renown, the *Academy of Motion Pictures* maintains a *Players Directory* (*www.PlayersDirectory.com*) with various levels of information on thousands of performers...many with direct contact information available online so you can bypass the agent!

But if you're really set on reaching out to a particular actor or actress, and the only contact information is for their agent, just remember to send a specific offer IN WRITING to be considered, including a specific offer of remuneration and/or reimbursement for travel expenses.

Here's an example...slightly edited from a sample letter Halbert suggested:

> *Dear Celebrity-Type Person,*
>
> *I am writing to you in care of your agency because I would like to invite you to speak at my organization/campaign's event in (city/town) on (date).*
>
> *Our budget for this speaking engagement is (amount), and we will also reimburse you for coach airfare and one night's stay at a local hotel.*
>
> *As I am working against a deadline, I need to hear from you by (date). Because of the time pressure, I am sending a copy of this letter to your personal manager and your talent agency, and I am leaving this message verbally with your answering service.*
>
> *Sincerely,*
>
> *Joe Candidate*

You can expand upon and change this as appropriate, but that's pretty much the gist of it. Now let's move your search to some simpler, greener pastures…

# IF YOU BELIEVE IN FREE SPEECH, GIVE ONE!

If you're a candidate or political organization, bagging a Hollywood celebrity isn't usually your first, or even best, option.

Indeed, let's say you're a Republican women's club trying to book a speaker for your annual fundraising dinner. In that case, the type of celebrity you'll be looking for will be someone high up the *political* food chain.

Like maybe a congressman or U.S. senator who has developed a little national name ID. Or the head of a national public policy organization – such as the National Rifle Association or the American Conservative Union.

And here's a great side benefit about focusing on booking political-type celebrities such as these…

> *1. If you're looking for an elected official, especially a member of Congress, they are not allowed to charge speaking fees any longer.*

At worst, you might have to cover their travel

23

expenses…but check campaign finance laws on this, too. Such laws are extremely complicated and change on a fairly regular basis. The Congress member's staff probably knows what's allowed and not allowed far better than you.

*2. Ditto heads of major conservative organizations.*

While they are not legally prohibited from charging speaking fees, many make public appearances for free as part of their mission to educate the public about their organization or issue. They consider public speaking to simply be part of what they're already paid to do.

Indeed, some organizations will actually cover the speaker's entire travel cost…though you'll likely have a better chance of booking someone *big* if you at least offer to pay for coach airfare and their hotel.

But, of course, before you can get anybody to even consider your invitation…they have to SEE IT!

# GETTING TO THE TOP OF THE PILE

Let's say you're a *nobody*.

*Don't be offended by the term. I was the biggest "nobody" you'd ever want to not know when I got started in politics in Nevada. I was a new resident managing a car rental operation at the airport who had never even heard of Harry Reid…and he sure as Hades had never heard of me!*

So let's say you're just starting out.

Let's say you're a first-time candidate, local party leader, club president or organization head without a lot of connections to movers-and-shakers.

Or maybe you're the program chair for your local women's club or Lincoln Day Dinner committee in search of a high-profile speaker that'll drive up ticket sales and attendance.

Indeed, let's say, for example, you'd like to get a popular U.S. senator to speak at your event. What do you do?

Or more to the point, what do MOST people do?

As often as not, the first thing they do is search Google for the phone number of the senator's office in Washington, DC.

At that point, they make a call and are passed along to the Senator's scheduler...whose primary job most often is to say *"No"* in as polite and courteous way as possible, especially if the invitation is to speak at an out-of-state event.

But rather than coming out and saying *"No"* on the phone, the scheduler is more likely going to ask you send him or her a WRITTEN request with the date and time of the event.

Right then and there this dissuades a large number of people who simply won't take the time and trouble of sending a formal written invitation.

But let's say you do send a nice invitation on your letterhead to the Senator's scheduler. Guess what happens to it?

It gets tossed into a pile with dozens, if not hundreds of other requests from all across the country. In other words, it gets buried because there's nothing unique about your request to make it stand out from the others that look and sound EXACTLY like yours.

Want to know how to make yours stand out from the rest?

Simple. DON'T MAKE YOURS LOOK LIKE THE REST!

Easier said than done, right?

Wrong. Here's what you do...

Remember the Rule of Reciprocity. If you want to get something, give something first.

As marketer Joe Polish advises, never ask someone to do something for you without doing something for them first – even if all you do is make them laugh or smile.

Or as the late, great sales guru Zig Ziglar put it:

> *"You can get everything in life you want if you will just help enough other people get what they want."*

Here are a couple of suggestions…

## PHONE INTERVIEWS & ARTICLES

Do you have a blog? If not, get one. Used correctly and creatively, it can be the most powerful tool in your campaign arsenal.

Then do a little research and find out what bills your senator or congressman is sponsoring or co-sponsoring...or what issues he's championing.

Then give him a little e-ink.

Write a blog post or column promoting the bill or issue. Then send the link to the senator...and his staff!

Believe me, congressional staffers are always appreciative of someone lending support to the boss. After all, that helps with job security!

This one little step will go a long way to boosting your name ID, in a positive way, in the senator's office. As such, follow up letters and requests will no longer be coming from a complete stranger, but a valued ALLY.

But let's say you don't consider yourself an accomplished writer...or you don't feel you know the issue well enough to speak authoritatively on it.  No sweat.

Do a recorded interview.

You don't have to know the answers; you just have to come up with a half-dozen or so good questions.  Then call the appropriate staffer – congressional folks all have press secretaries and/or communications directors – and say something along these lines…

> *"Hi, I'm Chuck Muth and I'm (running for office, run an organization, publish a blog) and have an interest in tax reform.  I read that Sen. Johnson introduced a bill that would reform our tax code.  Would it be possible to do a short, 10-minute recorded phone interview on the topic that I could have transcribed and posted on our website?"*

You'd be surprised at how many times you'll get the actual elected official to do such an interview even if you're not a big-time *mainstream media* publication.  At the very least, you'll likely get an interview with a top staffer from the elected official's office.

Now if you've never done this sort of thing before, I'm going to give you the three steps you need to follow to pull this off quickly, simply and inexpensively…

*1. You need to set up an account with a company where you can not only conference in people (sometimes you'll want to allow others, especially your major donors, to listen in on the call "live" as a thank you for their generous support), but record the phone call digitally, as well.*

The service I've used for years is FreeConferencing.com.  The operative word being "free."  But it's also a dependable, reliable, high-quality service.  There are others, but FreeConferencing.com has worked just fine for me.

Once your audience is on the phone, you simply hit the "Record" button from the website monitoring page and…ask your questions.

The interviewee will give you the answers.

You thank them. Save the recording.

And…you're done.

*2. Now you need to get your interview up on your blog.*

For a written transcript, I use *iDictate.com*.

All you do is upload your audio file from *FreeConferencing.com* to *iDictate.com*…and within a day or so, they'll send back a written transcription in a text document ready to simply copy and paste into your blog.

There is no charge to set up an account and no monthly fees. You only pay for the work you send them.

I usually conduct interviews of 45-60 minutes long and the cost generally runs in the neighborhood of a hundred bucks. So a short 10-15 minute interview will cost you chicken feed…especially compared to the value you could receive down the road.

Or if you have the time and but not the dough…painstakingly transcribe the interview yourself. A man's gotta do what a man's gotta do!

*Caution:* Dictation isn't always 100% accurate…especially if you're using "shop talk" and terms the transcriptionist isn't familiar with. So before you post your interview, read through it and make sure there are no typos or misspelled words, names, phrases, etc.

*3. As an additional side benefit, there are easy, inexpensive services you can use to post the actual audio of the actual interview into your blog, as well.*

I use a service called *AudioGenerator.com*.

With Audio Generator, I simply upload the recorded interview from FreeConferencing.com and Audio Generator saves the file and creates the code you (or your webmaster) can insert right into your blog so all people have to do is press *Play* and listen to the full interview.

There is a monthly fee for this service, so it's best that you use them if you're going to do interviews on a regular basis...which you SHOULD!

Look, even if the folks you interview never directly endorse your campaign or organization or speak at one of your events, the very fact that you INTERVIEWED them is de facto social proof that you're *somebody*.

Somebody of substance. Somebody with gravitas. Somebody to be reckoned with.

You, as the interviewer, gain credibility and can bask in the reflected glory of your interviewees. This is powerful stuff! Trust me...I've been doing this for years. And I absolutely started out as a one-man *nobody*.

In any event, after you've posted the interview on your blog or website, make sure you send a link to everyone on your email list...and especially to the person you interviewed and/or his or her staff. This will greatly help move you up to the top of the pile once you extend a written invitation asking for an endorsement or with a speaking request.

Will this technique work on everybody? *No.*

Will it work with a lot of people if you just do it often enough? *Oh, yeah.*

Remember what hockey great Wayne Gretzky said: *"You miss 100% of the shots you never take."*

# MAKE A DONATION FIRST

If you're in a position to do so, make a small contribution to the senator's campaign.

Think of it this way:

If you make a $200 donation to the campaign...and the senator comes out to do your event...and because of his appearance you raise $2,000.00 or $5,000.00 or $10,000.00 or more...

That'd be a pretty darned good return on investment, wouldn't it?!

And while some will whine and complain about *pay to play*, the simple reality is that donors are naturally given greater consideration over non-donors...and especially over complete strangers in another state.

Again, to get your request moved to the top of the pile instead of the bottom of the pile, it definitely will help if you're a known quantity as a supporter in one way or another.

Name recognition is a biggie.

But let's say you're pressed for time and want to get a speaking invitation out to Mr. Big without having an established relationship of some kind. Let's say you have no choice but to extend the invitation as a complete stranger. Here's what you do:

**DON'T** fax, email or snail-mail the traditional one-page letter of invitation that everybody else and their uncle is sending.

Stand out! Be creative! Send a PACKAGE, not just a letter.

I learned this technique from a pair of marketing geniuses named Brad and Alan Antin back in the 1990s. It works like a charm…

## SNEAKERS FOR SPEAKERS

Let's start with the *Foot in the Door* package…which I've used successfully on a number of occasions. While it didn't always land me the speaker, it never failed to get my invitation and follow-up calls answered.

Here's what you do…

First you find out the prospect's shoe size (or make an educated guess - but guess smaller than you think, not larger!), and go out and buy a nice pair of athletic shoes.

Then take one shoe out and gift-wrap the box in really nice gold foil paper.

Also inside the box put a letter of invitation that reads something like this…

*"Dear Mr. Big Shot,*

*"I'd very much like to invite you to speak at my organization's upcoming event, but being a complete stranger I didn't know how to make my invitation stand out from the dozens of requests I'm sure you get on a regular basis.*

*"That's why I'm sending you this shoe. It's my way of 'getting my foot in the door.'*

*"Our (event) is scheduled for (date) in (city/town). If you would be so kind as to accept our invitation, I'll bring you your other shoe when you arrive!*

*Sincerely,*

*Chuck Muth*

*P.S. If I've gotten your shoe size wrong, please have someone in your office let me know the correct size and I'll get it taken care of.*

Then have the package delivered via FedEx or UPS…or better yet, a special courier.

Do you think a speaking invitation like THAT is going to get noticed?

In the immortal words of Sarah Palin, *"You betcha!"*

Doesn't guarantee your invitation will be accepted, but pretty much guarantees it'll be received, noticed and considered.

Now, the tennis shoe package is pretty generic and can be used for just about anybody. But if you really do your homework and think creatively, you can put together an invitation package that is far more personal.

# THE SHERIFF JOE STORY

To give you an idea of what I'm talking about, here's a humorous story of an invitation package I sent back in the late 90's that worked...but caused a bit of panic in the Maricopa (Arizona) sheriff's office!

At the time I was working as a special projects consultant for the Nevada Republican Party and was in charge of getting well-known figures to headline fundraising events. As such, I wanted to get Sheriff Joe Arpaio to speak at an event in Reno.

Now in case you don't know, long before Sheriff Joe became known for his aggressive enforcement of Arizona's immigration laws, he was well-known for his less-than-hospitable treatment of prisoners in his custody.

They were housed in tents, not air-conditioned cells...which was especially uncomfortable during the summer months when temperatures reach into triple digits ...and were fed green bologna and forced to wear pink underwear.

No, there was no coddling of criminals by Sheriff Joe, which earned him the nickname, *America's Toughest Sheriff.*

It also earned him regular threats from various ne'er do wells who didn't take a liking to his brand of incarceration. Keep that in mind…

So instead of sending Sheriff Joe a *tennis shoe* invitation, I went over to the local Army surplus store to pick up something a bit more personal.

Most of you youngsters probably don't know this, but in the old days two-man *pup* tents came in two parts that snapped together. We used these often as a Boy Scout when I was growing up. One scout carried one half of the tent and the other carried the other half so that one person wasn't lugging the whole thing himself.

So I bought one of these tents – which weren't very expensive – and wrapped up one half in the box along with a note similar to the *tennis shoe* letter that basically said:

> *"I'm guessing you can always use another tent, so I'm sending half of one with this invitation. I'll give you the other half when you arrive in Reno."*

I put the letter of invitation in the box, sealed it, wrapped it and shipped it.

Oh, yeah. It got noticed. And Sheriff Joe spoke at our Reno fundraising event. But not without a little kerfuffle first…

You see, because of all the threats against the sheriff, his office staff called in the bomb squad folks to x-ray the package before they opened it!

Sheriff Joe has now spoken at three other events for me since then, one being for our First Friday Happy Hour event in Las Vegas in

May 2010. This was shortly after Arizona passed a new law cracking down on illegal immigration, and Sheriff Joe was right smack in the middle of the controversy.

While we normally were getting crowds of around 200-250 people at this monthly event, over 1,000 showed up that night to see Sheriff Joe…and that didn't even include all the protestors outside on the sidewalk!

On another occasion, I tried to book Charles Sykes, author of a book titled *Dumbing Down Our Kids*. Either in the book or in an interview, I can't remember which, Mr. Sykes referenced the *broken glass theory*.

In short, the theory was put forward by a pair of social scientists in the early '80s and was described in an *Atlantic Monthly* article as follows…

> *"Consider a building with a few broken windows. If the windows are not repaired, the tendency is for vandals to break a few more windows. Eventually, they may even break into the building, and if it's unoccupied, perhaps become squatters or light fires inside."*

The theory itself is not important for our purposes. The point is, Mr. Sykes referenced it. So…

I went out and bought a small window and broke the glass out of it. Had the window boxed up and gift-wrapped with the letter of invitation inside referencing the *broken glass*. And shipped it.

We didn't get Mr. Sykes as a speaker, but I'm certain the invitation was at least received and read.

The possibilities are endless…limited only by your imagination.

More?

OK, here's another one I've *swiped* from the Antin Brothers even though I haven't used it yet myself...

# ANCIENT PROVERB SAY

Pick up a bag of Chinese fortune cookies from your grocery store or local Chinese restaurant. Then take a pair of tweezers and ever-so-carefully remove the little white piece of paper with the fortune message on it.

Then replace the original fortune message with a new one of your own. Maybe try something like this:

*"Free speech is a wonderful thing. Give them often!"*

Now take the fortune cookie with your personal message inside and place it into a jewelry box...which you'll gift-wrap in gold foil paper.

Now in this case, put your letter of invitation inside a sealed envelope with the following on the outside:

*"Please open your gift before opening this envelope."*

Now place the envelope and the gift-wrapped jewel box inside another box and ship it to your targeted VIP speaker.

One more? OK, here's yet another adapted from the Antin Brothers (those guys were true creative geniuses!)...

46

# GET CROSS WITH THEM

Go out and buy a Cross pen and have your target's name engraved on it.

The engraving isn't necessary, but people LOVE to see their own names…and the personalization makes the gift that much more impressive.

You can purchase Cross pens online at *www.Cross.com* starting at around $25 plus just an additional $8 or so for engraving.

Cheap at the price if it results in a $1,000 donation or speaking gig, right?

You might include in your note something along the lines of…

> *"Please bring this Cross pen with you to sign autographs after your speech!"*

Or…

> *"The only thing better than signing a donation check to me/us is signing the check with a fine Cross pen!"*

Of course, it doesn't have to be an engraved Cross pen to make a great impression. All kinds of items can be engraved...from the fun, to the weird to the high-end. You can get some ideas by visiting...

*www.personalizationmall.com*

Or...

*www.ThingsRemembered.com*

Or just Google *engraved gifts*.

# HAPPY BIRTHDAY!

Whether you want to nurture an existing relationship or want to start one new with a VIP, if you have their birthday, you have an opportunity to make a big impression every year.

But if you're going to send them something, don't send just some commercial greeting card...though that alone will set you apart from most of the others who want something from *Mr. Big.*

Send something valuable, interesting, fun or cool. Something that'll stand out. Something that will almost FORCE them to remember you.

Joe Polish talks about sending people samurai statues. Weird. Who sends someone a statue of a samurai?

Exactly.

You'll stand out. You'll get noticed. You'll be remembered.

For high quality and highly-perceived value, it's hard to beat sending a gift pack from OmahaSteaks.com. Or if your prospect is known to be somewhat of an outdoor enthusiast, it's hard to beat *Orvis.com.*

Or send a *very* personalized gift basket; a themed basket that fits your prospect's interest.

For example, if you're prospect likes fishing, send a basket loaded with fishing items.

Whatever your prospect's interest, you can probably find a specific gift basket for them. Just Google *gift baskets for (insert interest)*. Fishermen. Hunters. Baseball fans. Runners. Music lovers. You name it.

By the way, a good source of high-quality general interest gift baskets at a decent price is *Overstocked.com*.

But if you're not sure of your target's hobbies or interests, buy some appropriate political items that would fit in a gift basket – books, DVD's, CD's, bumper stickers, t-shirts, caps, buttons, lapel pins, key chains, magnets, mouse pads, etc.

If you don't have a store that sells politically-oriented merchandise in your town, you can always shop online. Try *www.PoliticalGifts.com*. LOTS of stuff there.

Then just take all your items, along with a personalized card or note, and assemble them in a gift basket and ship to your prospect. Or if you have no gift basket talent, just take your items to a local florist and let them put it together for you.

## GOING HIGH-TECH

Whether included in a gift basket or sent as a stand-alone item, don't feel limited to conveying your message via printed letter alone. The cost of producing a CD or DVD to grab attention is relatively cheap these days.

Indeed, recording a simple digital audio or video message can be easily accomplished these days on your PC, laptop, tablet or smart-phone. You're not looking for a slick, Hollywood-quality production; just a simple, personal "sales" message to a potential customer or donor.

> *"Hi, this is Chuck Muth, president of Citizen Outreach, and if you're like me, you're frustrated with…"*

As with a fundraising or sales letter, the message has to be strong and compelling, but the production itself doesn't have to be of Cecil B. DeMille-like epic proportions. You can sit at your desk, look into your laptop or tablet camera and hit *record.*

Once you get your audio or video message recorded, you need to decide how to deliver it. And yes, it's a lot cheaper to download the recording on a website and then try to drive people there to view or hear it.

Cheaper, yes. More effective, no.

You'll make a far better impression and get noticed by physically putting something in their hands. That means burning your audio or video recording onto a CD or DVD...something fairly easily accomplished on just about every home computer these days, at least in small quantities.

You'll still want to include a letter or note with the CD or DVD that you mail to a prospect, but instead of telling your entire story in print, the sole purpose of your letter or note is simply to get the person to listen to the CD or watch the DVD.

That's it. The basics anyway. Ready to get a little more creative?

# THE LONE RANGER TECHNIQUE

I learned this one from a promotion the good folks at Glazer-Kennedy did for a high-priced marketing conference ($2,997) - their annual Info-Summit.

What they did was take an old, copyright-free episode of the Lone Ranger radio program, downloaded it, recorded and inserted their own commercials for the Info-Summit…and then burned it onto CD's.

You can pretty much use any copyright-free radio program from the 30's, 40's or 50's.

*The Adventures of Sam Spade. The Shadow. Death Valley Days. Hopalong Cassidy. Fibber McGee & Molly. Abbott & Costello. Flash Gordon. Buck Rogers. Ozzie & Harriet. Red Skelton. Superman. Blondie. Jack Benny. The Thin Man. Gunsmoke. Perry Mason. Groucho Marx. Sherlock Holmes.*

These are easy to find and easy to download. Just Google *copyright-free old time radio* and you'll find multiple sources.

Of course, using shows from *The Golden Age of Radio* will especially resonate with older prospects. But it's really not about the show itself you choose to send; it's the simple idea of embedding your sales message into an old-time radio program.

Who does such a thing? I'm betting NOT your competitors!

Want to make an even bigger splash. Don't just send the CD. Send a CD player…with the CD already loaded in!

CD players today are very inexpensive. So rather than hope your prospect will have a CD player in his home or office, or will remember to play it in his car on the way home, all the recipient will have to do is open your box or envelope, turn on the power and hit *Play*.

And of course this technique isn't just for selling conferences or other high-end products or services; it can be used by non-profit organizations or political campaigns seeking high-dollar donors.

In fact, you don't even have to go through the trouble of inserting a fundraising pitch into the program in place of the commercials. You can simply record a 2-3 minute introduction and slap it on the front-end of the show.

> *"Hello, this is Chuck Muth, candidate for Congress. It doesn't take Sherlock Holmes to figure out who's killing the American economy in Washington. It's elementary. The first clue is…*
>
> *"Blah, blah, blah…*
>
> *"So I hope you'll consider investing in my campaign. Now sit back, relax and travel back in time to enjoy this 1946 radio broadcast of Sherlock Holmes and the Mystery of the Vanishing White Elephant."*

All you have to do is find any kind of tie-in, no matter how thin, between what you're trying to sell or market and some old-time radio show...and you're in business. The prospect doesn't even have to listen to the show itself.

Now as for videos...

# LIGHTS, IPHONES, ACTION!

Probably the most powerful thing you can do with a video is to self-produce a short introductory message about you, your company, your campaign or your organization…followed by:

> *"But don't take my word for it, take theirs…"*

And then show 3-5 minutes of people saying great things about you on camera!

Testimonials and endorsements by real people in their own words is *social proof* worth its weight in gold. And it's never been easier or more convenient to do.

Let's say you give a speech at a local community club or home owner's association. After the speech a lady comes up and says how much she loved what you had to say and how she wants you to get elected. Here's what you say…

> *"That's very kind of you to say and it'd be a huge help if I could share what you just said with others who couldn't be here tonight. Would you mind repeating what you just told me while I record it on my iPhone?"*

It doesn't get much easier than that.

And the best thing is...*it's real.* The person shouting your praises isn't acting or making it up. And they're communicating how they feel in the heat of the moment, when their emotions are highest and most genuine.

Record these short video testimonials wherever you go...including door-to-door campaigning.

Again, the objective here isn't to produce something slick. Keep it simple. Keep it real.

Use your best video testimonials and endorsements in a sort of *demo reel* with minimal Hollywood production values other than good lighting, good sound and good framing.

But even if not a *testimonial* video, whatever you produce will more likely be watched if it's included in some kind of *shock and awe* package like we've been describing above.

Here's another idea I've *swiped* from the good folks at Glazer-Kennedy.

First you produce your video. Then you put the video inside a portable DVD player. Then box the DVD player with your video already loaded inside a box labeled *Perishable, Open Immediately.*

Also in the box you'll include a nice linen dinner napkin, a nice serving plate and a nice dinner fork. All of which, you'll explain in the enclosed note, should be used to...eat the gourmet dessert you've also enclosed while watching the video!

What kind of dessert?

Well, just about anything you can find that can be shipped overnight will suffice, but consider this suggestion from Omaha Steaks:

> *"Our rich and seductive Chocolate Lover's Cake draws rave reviews from even the most seasoned chocoholics! A red rose adorns the top of the cake and chocolate shavings decorate the sides. Moist, indulgent and full of flavor, for an unforgettable finale to your most elegant meals."*

Of course, the problem here is you'll first have to have Omaha Steaks overnight the cake to you…and then re-package the cake with your DVD player and note.

So the other option will be to find a local gourmet bakery or restaurant that can ship desserts overnight and will package your DVD player with their treat.

And by the way, the most important aspect of all these ideas is to GET THE PACKAGE OPENED…the sooner the better.

And the big (and truthful) warning label on the outside that reads PERISHABLE is about as effective as anything else you could possible do!

# FINAL THOUGHTS

The most important thing to remember here is that you'll be much more successful in getting support from folks you already have some kind of ongoing relationship with than *cold-calling* them as a complete stranger.

Build rapport. Do something *for* them first.

And be fun.

Most of the folks you'll be targeting with these efforts are in high-pressure, high-stress positions. Anything and anyone who can lighten their day will be a welcome interruption.

Also, be creative. Be different. Stand out.

With rare exceptions, most of your prospect's employees and staffers are probably not very creative. They don't like to stick their necks out. They don't like to take chances.

Which is probably one of the reasons they're an employee and not an employer!

In any event, seeing true out-of-the-box creativity isn't something they're used to. So again, you'll stand out. You'll get attention.

Secondly, get connected to connected people.

If you're not in the *inner circle* where the big fish swim, find someone who is. It's one thing to call *Mr. Big* out of the blue and ask for a favor, interview, speaking engagement or donation.

It's another thing altogether to have someone you know make an introduction and vouch for you to someone you want to know.

Or better yet, partner up with somebody with far better name ID and connections than you and share the spotlight.

For example, in starting my *Conservative Leadership Conference*, I invited Grover Norquist, president of *Americans for Tax Reform*, to be the event's co-sponsor.

Not only did it help give the event instant credibility – since no one had ever heard of me, but everyone had heard of Grover – but Grover had contact information and connections to many speakers who never would have given me the time of day otherwise.

Along those same lines, look for an Honorary Chairman for your event.

In the first year of our *Conservative Leadership Conference*, then-Rep. John Shadegg agreed to be our Honorary Chairman and allowed us to send out invitations under his name.

People who otherwise wouldn't have opened an email invitation *from Chuck Muth* immediately opened up the exact same invitation *from Congressman John Shadegg*. And Rep. Shadegg was proud and happy to help boost the conservative movement in any way he could.

So don't be afraid to share the credit and rewards with others who can help make your events a bigger success. Remember what Ronald Reagan said:

> *"There is no limit to the amount of good you can do if you don't care who gets the credit."*

This last piece of advice goes without saying – so naturally, I'm going to say it:

Always say *please* and *thank you*. Often.

It's amazing how seldom this is done in society today.

And after someone has done you a favor…even if it's just talking to you on the phone or exchanging a few emails…get their snail-mail address and send them a HAND-WRITTEN thank you card.

So few people do this any longer that those notes *really* stand out.

That said, THANK YOU for taking time to read this book.

And *please* email me any comments, suggestions or questions to *chuck@campaigndoctor.com*. Better yet, if you find a new idea or tactic to successfully get past the gatekeeper, let me know so I can continue to update and improve *Getting Past the Gatekeeper* in the future.

Now…

Once you get past the gatekeeper and you're in front of Mr. Big…what do you do?

To that end I'm including the following two bonus chapters to help you write more effective letters and/or make more effective phone or in-person calls on important and influential people.

Onward…

# ONE-ON-ONE FUNDRAISING

In the beginning stages of your campaign, probably 70% of your time should be spent asking for money. Get it in the bank NOW.

At the end of the campaign, the bulk of your time should be devoted to asking for votes, not checks. Ten dollars raised in March is probably worth $100 raised in October ... or more.

Except for candidates in high profile races, it's probably not cost-effective to start a direct mail fundraising program. Unless your campaign has a very special *hook* or an already-established *house* file, the printing and postage cost likely precludes you from using direct mail profitably.

(Read the following bonus chapter *"17 Secrets to Direct Mail Fundraising"* if direct mail *is* something your campaign is interested in).

Fundraising events - such as dinners, receptions, BBQ's, etc. - take a lot of time, planning and preparation. If *someone else* is willing to spend that time, fine. But this is NOT the best use of the candidate's time. Especially if you're not well known.

One-on-one, in-person solicitations from major donors is a good use of a candidate's time ... just make sure the potential contribution is worth it. One-on-one is not a cost effective way to raise $25 donations.

Now, if you're a conservative candidate, here's a look at what your typical donor (not necessarily voter) probably will look like:

*Average age is 69-70 years old.* This makes sense since most people in their 30's and 40's are still making mortgage payments, car payments and putting kids through school. Their "disposable" income is at a premium ... which means they don't have much "extra" sitting around to give to political causes and candidates.

*2/3 are men.* Sorry, ladies. This statistic is changing slowly in each election cycle, as more and more women make their own political contributions. But for now, the lion's share of GOP donors are still of the gender from Mars, not Venus.

*About 90% are homeowners.*

*2/3 are retired.*

*Their average income is $50,000 a year.*

*They are highly educated. 70% have at least some college.*

*60-70% are married. 20% are widowed.*

*Over 50% have served in the military.*

*75% regularly give to charities.*

Most importantly, however, is their level of interest in politics and their philosophical leanings.

The average conservative donor is extremely well-informed. They read the papers, watch the news programs and listen to talk radio. They're also conservative ... not *moderate*.

So, although your campaign may decide to appeal to the 32-year-old, working single mother living in an apartment who barely has two nickels to rub together for her VOTE, this is NOT a demographic you should devote much time or attention to when it comes to fundraising.

Now, where do you find the people who are most likely to give you a donation?

Well, the best place to start looking is among people who have already given a political contribution in the past, particularly people who have given to a campaign or organization similar to yours. And the place to find this list of potential prospects are the campaign finance reports filed by candidates with their local election department or secretary of state.

**WARNING**: Check the laws in your community FIRST to be sure this is allowed.

For example, you may NOT use the campaign finance reports of congressional candidates which are filed with the Federal Elections Commission for the purpose of fundraising. Make sure a similar prohibition does not exist for your local community or state. *(Of course, if a congressional candidate is willing to provide you his or her list themselves, that's a different story.)*

Now, if those public records ARE available and ARE usable, then start pulling them immediately. In most cases, these reports will give you the names, addresses and phone numbers of the various contributors - as well as the amount of money they gave.

In general, if you're a Republican candidate pull the reports of all high-profile, well-financed Republican candidates who ran in the past couple of elections, especially the Republican who last ran for the seat you're now seeking.

Talk about a target rich environment.

If you see that Bob Smith gave $500 to GOP candidate Fred Jones in the last election cycle, then you definitely want to find a way to talk with Mr. Smith. He has the ability to give a large donation, an exhibited willingness to make such a donation to a political cause ... and you know where to contact him.

It doesn't get any better than that.

But before we get to the best way to make contact with the Mr. Smiths of the political world, here are some additional sources of prospects for you to consider:

- *Your own rolodex and Christmas card list*
- *Lobbyist directory*
- *Chamber of Commerce and other business lists*
- *Association directories and newsletters*
- *Charitable lists*
- *Voter file*

The voter file is probably the worst list to use to find donor prospects. But if that's all you've got, use it. To increase your success rate, though, try focusing your search on registered voters who vote in the primaries (hard-core partisans) - not just the general elections - and are over 50 years of age and living in their own homes in upscale neighborhoods.

Once you begin collecting names of potential prospects, you should have someone in the campaign add them into a computer database. For that matter, all this research work and preparation should be done by your campaign manager, finance director, staffer or campaign volunteer - NOT you, the candidate. Your job is to ask for the money, not compile the list and do data input.

OK. Before you start asking for money from your list, you still need to do two things:

*1. Prepare a one-page summary of your political plan*
*2. Prepare a one-page campaign budget*

Generally speaking, all donors are going to be asking you pretty much the same questions before giving you a check. Here are the Top 10 most commonly-asked questions you'll likely get in any fundraising solicitation, be it over the phone, in person or through the mail...

*1. Why are you running?*

This is probably the most frequently-asked question by potential donors and voters alike ... and you'd better have a pretty powerful, standard answer ready at the switch. You should be able to articulate your answer in 30 seconds or less. Any longer ... and you probably need to think this question ... and your answer ... through a little more. In fact, your answer to this question should definitely be written down and memorized.

*2. How do you expect to win?*

This is supposed to be the essence of your written campaign plan. While you need not reveal the confidential, in-house strategies your campaign is considering, you should be able to paint a broad-based synopsis of the overall, general strategy ... including your message strategy.

*3. How many votes will it take to win?*

When asked this question, be prepared to give an exact number ... not some *guess* or *gut feeling* ... and be able to explain how you came up with that number. This will show that you and your campaign know what you're doing and aren't just *flying by the seat of your pants.*

*4. Where will your votes come from?*

Again, using established formulas you'll be able to determine exactly how many votes you can reasonably expect to get out of each and every precinct in your district. Based on your individual campaign, you may need to tweak those numbers to allow for conditions specific to your particular race.

But again, being able to tell a potential donor exactly how many votes you need to get from each and every precinct in your district will show you aren't some well-intentioned rube who just fell off the turnip truck last night.

*5. How much money have you raised so far?*

Money follows money. Being able to show a potential donor that others have already coughed up for your campaign will alleviate their fear of being the only *sucker* backing a nag in your political race. So make sure you hit up all your friends, family and co-workers early on to *stake* your campaign before going after contributions from strangers and the *professional* donor community.

And don't forget to put your own *skin* in the pot ... regardless of how much it is. Why should a complete stranger invest in your campaign if even you don't have enough confidence to put your own money into it?

> *As a side note: If you're thinking/hoping the party or some other entity/organization is going to fully fund your race, you're whistlin' Dixie. The party folks have their own fundraising problems to deal with.*

No, the responsibility for raising your campaign cash rests with you, the candidate, and you alone.

*6. How much will your campaign cost?*

Again, if you've prepared a written campaign budget you'll have this figure at your fingertips. Your campaign budget should include cost estimates for such things as: staff, consultants, signage, headquarters, flyers, direct mail, TV, radio, postage, printing, phones, etc.

*7. How do you expect to raise it?*

Do you know the answer to this question? If not, you probably don't have a written Finance Plan.

Your *Finance Plan* tells you where you expect to get the money to fund your Campaign Plan's budget.

- How much are you putting in?
- How much is realistically coming from the party and other affiliated organizations?
- How much do you expect to raise from major donors (e.g., $20,000 from 20 persons contributing $1,000 each)?

- How much from various fundraising events (e.g., $10,000 from 20 neighborhood house parties netting $500 each)?
- How much from direct mail?
- How much from phone calls?
- How much directly from your finance committee?
- Etc.

*8. Who's supporting/working on your campaign?*

Although you may not be well-known to the political *establishment*, endorsements by community and political leaders go a long way to lending your campaign the legitimacy needed to attract financial support.

In addition, the presence of some highly-respected political professionals working for your campaign generates donor confidence as well, and will enable you to raise money which otherwise wouldn't flow your way.

*9. What are you going to do differently from others who have run in this race and lost?*

Good question. Because if you're just going to run the same, boring, stale campaign with no life, no money and no volunteers as the last person who got their head kicked in by your opponent ... why, oh why, would a donor want to flush his hard-earned cash down the crapper by giving it to you?

Final Answer: He won't.

If you can't explain how you're going to do something significantly different from those who have run and lost in the past ... you won't need a bookkeeper for your campaign. Your toes will suffice.

*10. Are you going to campaign full time?*

This is an important question for many folks. They're looking for serious commitment *from* you before they make a serious commitment *to* you - that is, donate cash to your campaign.

Of course, not everyone can quit their day job to run for office. But even if you can't campaign full-time, you need to be able to show that the campaign itself will be in operation full-time ... even when you're not there. Be prepared to explain what campaign staffers, volunteers and activists will be doing full-time while you're out putting bread and butter on the table for your family.

These questions are likely to come up whether you are *dialing for dollars* or soliciting the donor in person. Be prepared to answer them.

That brings us to your budget.

Telling a prospective donor you need, *"Oh, around $50,000"* ain't gonna cut it. That tells the donor you haven't really done your homework.

If he or she is smart, they'll ask you to break that down for them - item by item - and if you want so much as a nickel from them, you better be able to do it.

Of course, every campaign is different, but if you've never developed a campaign budget before, here are some campaign expenses you probably have to consider for inclusion:

- *Photography*
- *Walk cards/campaign brochures*
- *Yard signs*
- *Direct mail pieces*

- *Newspaper ads*
- *TV and/or radio*
- *Get-Out-The-Vote mailers/phones*
- *Rent and utilities for a headquarters*
- *Salaries and consulting fees*
- *Travel expenses*
- *Telephones*
- *Office supplies and equipment*

Armed with the reason why you're running, how you're going to run and what it's expected to cost, you are now prepared to actually begin raising the money.

The most time-efficient way to raise small- and medium-sized donations is to call people on the phone and ask. The most effective way to raise large donations is in person. And getting money from the *big fish* usually requires a personal visit from the *big cheese*. That means the candidate himself - or the party chairman or club president.

The good news is, once you get a meeting with a major donor - if you've done your homework, have a solid campaign plan and realistic budget - getting a check really isn't that tough.

The bad news is, getting that one-on-one meeting is the true hard part.

As discussed in the beginning of this book, there's the gatekeeper - the personal secretary or assistant whose job it is to keep you away from the boss. So common-sense says: *Be nice to the gatekeeper!*

Unless you are an incumbent or a high-profile, already-well-known candidate, chances are *Mr. Big* and his gatekeeper have no interest in giving you a sit-down. Unknown candidates with no name recognition making a fundraising *cold call* are about as welcome to major donors - who get hit up all the time by wacky candidates - as a skunk at a picnic.

Unless…

Unless you have an introduction.

This, ladies and gentlemen, is the true secret to a successful *finance committee*.

Sure, if you can put together a finance committee of people who will aggressively go out and raise money for you … great. Just keep feeding them names of prospects and cut 'em loose.

But if you're starting from scratch with people who haven't done campaign fundraising before, you're going to have to approach this process in a different fashion.

Again, you as the candidate or organization leader must be the one asking for the donation … and the hardest part is just getting your foot in the door. So the real value of a finance committee for most campaigns isn't so much asking for money … but *greasing the skids* for you to get an audience with Mr. Big.

It's just this simple. Which of these two approaches has the best chance of getting an appointment with Mr. Big?

> *"Hello, I'm Joe Candidate and I'd like an appointment to talk to you about donating to my campaign."*

Or this call from a friend of *Mr. Big's*:

> *"Hi, Bob. I'm working with Joe Candidate and he's really a good guy who I think you should meet with him."*

Bingo. Like your daddy always told you, it's who you know, not what you know.

The personal *connection* linking you, the candidate or chairman, to the potential major donor has a MUCH better chance of getting you past the gatekeeper and in front of *Mr. Big.*

After that, the ball's in your court.

So ... the smart candidate will use his novice finance committee to unearth *connections* that can be used to get appointments ... not necessarily to get checks.

Your objective, writes Dr. Jeffrey Lant in his excellent fundraising book, *Development Today*, should be to recruit a team of 15-20 people who will regularly review potential donor lists with you and identify any connections. They should also be prepared to give you any personal information about the prospect which may help you find some *common ground* with the prospect. Information such as:

- *Where they grew up*
- *Where they went to school*
- *Their hobbies*
- *Their military experience*
- *Their family*
- *Their religious affiliations*
- *Charities he/she supports*
- *How much he/she might give*
- *The best way to approach him/her*
- *And especially hot button political issues*

Once in a while, you'll land yourself a real go-getter on your finance committee who will recognize a name and say, *"Hey, I know Mr. Big. Let me call him and ask for $500 for you."*

If you get that out of a finance committee member, great. But if not, Lant advises that you try to at least get one of the following...

> *"I know Mr. Big. Let me call and schedule an appointment for us. I'll go with you and follow up, if need be, after the meeting.*

> *"I know Mr. Big and can schedule an appointment but can't go with you. I'll also make a follow-up call after your meeting if necessary."*

> *"I'll make an appointment for you, but that's it."*

> *"I won't call for you, but you can use my name."*

The key is to get a wide variety of people on your finance committee who will meet with you regularly - in person or by phone/fax/e-mail - to review a constantly updated potential major donor list and let you know if they have any *connection* which will help you get an appointment.

To cast the widest net possible and greatly improve your chances of making a *connection*, you'll want to have as many of the following people as possible represented on your finance committee...

- *At least one representative from your community's largest corporate employer(s)*
- *A small business owner - preferably a printer (they know everybody!)*
- *A banker or a trust officer*
- *A lawyer (preferably one who will handle the campaign's legal work pro-*

*bono)*

- *An accountant (but someone OTHER than your campaign's treasurer)*
- *A leading lobbyist*
- *A media or PR expert*
- *Leaders from various professional groups, such as: doctors, real estate agents, developers, architects, dentists, etc.*

This will give your campaign the best chance of having someone on your finance committee knowing the prospect - or knowing someone who knows the prospect - and can get your foot in the door.

OK. Once you get a one-on-one appointment with Mr. Big, what do you do and say?

First, take someone else with you from your campaign if your *connection* won't be there. Arrive early. Dress respectfully. Start the meeting with a little social conversation. It's OK to tell the prospect that you're nervous and don't like asking for money...but that the cause is so important you must ask.

Explain why you are running and what you hope to achieve. Show the prospective donor your one-page budget. Give him a minute to peruse it, then ask if he/she has any questions.

LISTEN.

After answering the questions, look the donor right in the eye and say: *"I'm hoping you'd consider helping our campaign with this budget."* Then...

SHUT UP.

The donor will respond in one of three ways.

1. He or she might break out the checkbook right then and there and write you a donation.
2. He or she might say they're sorry, but can't help you.
3. Most often, however, he or she will say something along the lines of, *"How much are you looking for?"*

Of course, if you're prepared and have done your homework, you'll immediately spit out the appropriate figure.

Once the prospect asks *"how much,"* the hard part is done. You're most likely going to get something - the amount is just a final detail to be ironed out.

Still, your work isn't finished at this point. If you really want to be successful at fundraising, you need to go one more step:

> *"Sir, there's one other thing you could do to help. Could you refer me to some others who might be interested in our campaign?"*

That's right. Don't just ask for the donation ... ask for the Rolodex as well. About a third of donors will give you additional names ... and some will actually make appointment calls for you.

Let's wrap up with the single-most important aspect of successful fundraising: *saying thank you.*

Regardless of the amount contributed - whether it's one dollar or ten thousand dollars - you should send a thank you note of some kind within 48 hours max. Not only is it good manners ... it's good business. A donor who knows you truly value and appreciate his support is much more likely to provide it again ... for your re-election!

Now, for most down-ballot campaigns the most cost-effective and time-effective way to raise money will be...DIALING FOR DOLLARS.

Indeed, the best, most-effective use of your time early in your campaign is sitting in front of Alexander Graham Bell's invention and letting your fingers do the walking.

In fact, if you get really organized, you can have a volunteer do the actual dialing ... and hand the call off to you only once a *live* prospect is on the line. And while you're talking to that prospect, the volunteer is busy dialing the next number.

Time is your most valuable resource. Use it wisely.

*Dialing for Dollars* is a numbers game. The more people you call, the more money you raise... period.

So, what do you say to the prospect once you get him or her on the line?

*Introduce yourself, tell them the office you are running for ... and why you are running*. Since this question is on the donor's mind anyway, you may as well put it out on the table from the get-go.

*Tell the potential donor how much money you need to raise and what you'll be spending it on*. Again, these questions are very likely to be brought up in any solicitation, so you may as well provide the answers right up front.

*Explain why it is necessary to raise the money now*. Not tomorrow. Not next week. Not next month. NOW!

*Ask for a specific amount.* Don't force the donor to *guess* what the appropriate amount is.

*Once you make your pitch, stop talking.* If the donor has any questions, he or she will ask them. But if you just keep on talking, you're more likely to talk yourself right out of the donation.

It's natural to be nervous ... especially when you're new at this. And nervous people tend to ramble on and on and on and on. If you find yourself in the middle of doing this...just shut up as quickly as possible.

*Pick up the check.* Have a "*bag man*" go directly to the donor immediately. That way you eliminate the chance that the donor will procrastinate or forget to mail your check...or that the post office will lose it!

Now here's your payoff...

If you call 15 potential donors an hour, you should connect with seven.

On a good day, you will get money from four.

With an average donation of $100 each, you would raise $400 an hour.

That's $1,200 per day if you only devote three hours a day to dialing-for-dollars.

That comes to $3,600 a week if you only dial-for-dollars three days a week.

And that comes to $14,400 per month ... which ain't chicken-feed for many down-ballot races.

In fact, if you start in the early spring, you'll put between $75,000 and $100,000 in your account by *crunch time* in late September.

Many a campaign has been won with much less. And if you need more money, just spend more hours and days on the phone...or ask for larger donations.

Yes you will get rejected...often. Rejection is a hard thing to take. Get used to it.

You're the one who wanted to run for office. Having doors slammed in your face and phones slammed in your ear is part of the territory.

But don't get discouraged. This is a pure numbers game. The more calls you make, the more money you'll raise...period.

And the more you raise, the more things you can do to win your race.

So set up your dialing-for-dollars schedule NOW and get started.

As the kids say: *Just do it!*

# 17 SECRETS
## TO DIRECT MAIL FUNDRAISING

Other direct mail gurus will *sell you the sizzle* when it comes to direct mail tips...but I'm about to serve up the steak! So...let's bypass the pleasantries and get right down to business.

Whether you're trying to raise millions for a congressional or gubernatorial campaign ... or just a few thousand for a local race ... direct mail can and should be a key component of your fundraising plan. Done correctly, it can generate all the money you need to fund certain projects.

But...done poorly it can bankrupt you in a heartbeat!

A well-written and designed direct mail piece can sometimes do well even when mailed to a mediocre list of potential donors - but a lousy direct mail piece will flop, even to the greatest list on earth. With that said, here are 17 suggestions which will help dramatically improve your direct mail fundraising success.

Bear in mind, unlike the Ten Commandments, these suggestions aren't carved in stone. There are exceptions to every rule. But for the most part, sticking to the basics as outlined herein will serve you very well.

## SECRET #1: SELECTING THE RIGHT LIST

Who you mail to will be the greatest determining factor in the success of your direct mail project. Mailing to people who have already given to you before - your *house file* - or, at least, to a cause, campaign or candidate similar to yours - will net a far better response rate than, say, mailing randomly to a voter file.

While it is unlawful to use the contributor lists compiled by the Federal Elections Commission (FEC) for congressional and presidential candidates, many states allow you to mail fundraising letters to contributors to other state and local candidates. You might, for example, try mailing to people from your district or county who gave to your party's gubernatorial candidate - or other statewide candidates - in the last election. But check your local laws carefully before using such lists.

## SECRET #2: THE SIGNER

A direct mail appeal on your behalf which is signed by a governor, U.S. Senator, mayor or popular congressional representative will be much more powerful than if the letter is signed by an unknown county party chairman or first-time candidate. The signature of a celebrity or sports figure is also very powerful - often even more so than an elected official.

How much do you think actor Charlton Heston's signature was worth to the National Rifle Association? Put your personal ego aside and look for the biggest name you can find to sign your letters.

## SECRET #3: PREPARATION

Writing compelling and motivational copy is one of the most challenging and mind-draining experiences there is. I'm constantly amazed at people who think drafting a press release, a brochure or a direct mail appeal occurs at the snap of one's fingers. I literally spend hours upon hours on some projects just coming up with the right headline or first sentence.

While copywriting isn't rocket science, it ain't for the faint of heart either. Writing copy requires commitment and advance preparation. When you know you have to write something substantial, follow these simple preparation guidelines:

- *Make sure you are well-rested.*
- *Start early in the morning.*
- *Eliminate any chance of distraction. Turn off the phones and close the door.*
- *Eat lightly. Heavy meals make brain cells lazy.*

Don't worry if *writer's block* sets in and you find it difficult to begin or continue. This happens to everyone who's ever tried to write a letter to their aunt. Sometimes it will help clear the mind if you just walk away from the project for a while.

But more often than not, the best way to break writer's block is to simply start writing - anything. Don't worry about whether what you're writing is exactly what you want to say - or even anywhere near it. Just start writing. Write, write, write. Do it. Do it now.

The effort alone will almost always result in giving you a new idea or showing you the direction you should go in. As Gary Halbert, a bona fide direct mail *guru*, was fond of saying, *"More answers are found through movement than will ever be found through meditation."*

## SECRET #4: BECOME A COPYCAT

Don't try to reinvent the wheel - especially if you're just starting out in direct mail fundraising. All of that *junk mail* you've been throwing out for years should now be considered *research*. Instead to trashing direct mail appeals you receive, begin keeping a *swipe* file of direct mail samples which catch your attention. You can refer to them whenever you need to *swipe* an idea.

Now...there's a difference between being a copycat and a plagiarist. You can't take someone else's direct mail letter, copy it word-for-word, slap your name on it and send it back out to your own list. That's not only unethical; it's against the law.

However, as an exercise, Halbert suggested that novice copywriters take a successful direct mail letter and re-write it, word-for-word, on a yellow legal pad. This exercise will help you understand the thought process the original author went through and will dramatically improve your own copywriting skills.

The things you can and want to *swipe* from other direct mail pieces are ideas and package composition. Unless you're a really big player in direct mail, you probably don't have the time, the resources or the money to fully test your direct mail letters. The big boys aren't shy about mailing 10,000 letters each to two groups of people from the same list and changing only the color of the paper - testing to see which pulls the better response.

That's not practical for the average person.

Imitating and duplicating certain layouts and designs of successful direct mail organizations which have the deep pockets to fully test every piece is the quickest and least expensive way to assure your project has the best chance of success.

Look for things such as the size of the envelope and the texture of the paper. Is the letter done in one color, two colors or four colors? Does the package include a *lift* letter or a *grabber* (more on these later)? What kind of response form is used? How is everything laid out? What type-size is used? Was it mailed first-class or bulk-rate? Etc.

If you're writing for a conservative organization, one of the best investments you can make is sending $10 to the Republican National Committee (310 First Street, S.E., Washington, DC, 20003). From that point on, you'll get regular, high-quality, high-impact, well-researched direct mail solicitations which you can model for your own efforts.

The investment of $10 to get on the above list is worth every penny.

## SECRET #5: GETTING YOUR ENVELOPE OPENED

Halbert explained that most people, when opening their mail, unconsciously separate it into two piles: the "A" pile and the "B" pile.

The "A" pile contains mail that is generally considered important: a letter from mom, a rebate check, or a notice from the IRS.

The "B" pile consists of not-so-important correspondence - what is often referred to as *junk mail.*

Quite a few letters in the "B" pile get tossed in the garbage without ever being opened. So whatever you can do to make sure your letter finds its way into the "A" pile - by making it look as personal as possible - will be well worth your time and money.

Here are a few suggestions…

- *Mail first class and use a "live" first-class stamp. Don't meter your mail.*
- *If you decide to mail at the bulk-rate, again use a live bulk-rate stamp rather than an imprint of your postal permit number.*
- *Use a standard #10 business envelope. Personal stationary envelopes are even better. "Priority" envelopes are often best.*
- *Address the envelope using a courier, typewritten-style font. Handwritten is even better.*

As for the use "teaser copy" - such as "Your Help Is Urgently Requested" - on the outside of the envelope, experts disagree.

Halbert didn't like the use of teaser copy, maintaining that this tips your hand before the envelope ever gets opened.

Others say a compelling "teaser" on the outside of the envelope actually boosts interests and causes more people to open your envelope.

As with any such disagreements, the correct answer is: test.

Send half your envelopes with teaser copy and half without – coding each on the reply device so you can track response. Then see if one method pulls better than the other. If so, you have your answer.

Again, test, test, test, test. Take nothing for granted.

## SECRET #6: HEADLINES

Generally speaking, people read direct mail letters in the following order: the top of the first page, the signature, and then the P.S. What they're looking for is some indication that what your letter has to offer is something that will be of interest to them; a reason to sit down and read the whole *pitch*.

People are naturally tuned in to WIFM-radio..."*What's In it For Me?*"

So...if they open an envelope and the first thing they see is the name of YOUR organization or candidate, this immediately tells the reader that the most important thing to you is, well...YOU...and not the reader. This doesn't get you off on the right foot.

For most candidates and organizations, putting your name at the top of the first page serves no purpose other than ego-gratification. If you are so desperate for a daily boost to your self-esteem, get a dog. The purpose of a direct mail fundraising appeal is to raise money, not make you feel good about yourself.

Take your name off the top of your letter. You can always list your name and fancy logo at the end.

What you really want to do is get the reader immediately interested in hearing what you have to say - and want to continue reading further. To do that, you must start off with a compelling headline which will generate interest.

For the life of me, I don't know why so few people refuse to recognize the importance of leading a direct mail letter with a headline. The Libertarian Party is the only political organization I've come across that regularly leads their direct mail appeals with a headline instead of its logo.

Of course, they're extremely ingenious in how they do it. They include their name in the headline. Smart! Very smart.

Every article in every newspaper or magazine has a headline. The best headlines reach out and grab the reader's attention and pulls him into the story. Why should a direct mail letter be any different?

The most successful direct mail letter I ever produced while working for the Nevada GOP in the late 90s centered on labor union involvement in politics. It opened with the headline: *"Are Today's Big Labor Union Bosses the Mike Tysons of American Politics?"*

A compelling - if not slightly out of the ordinary - question. It evoked a visual image in some people's minds of AFL-CIO president John Sweeney taking a chunk out of Newt Gingrich's ear - as Tyson had done to Evander Holyfield in that infamous boxing fiasco held in Las Vegas.

People thought about *cheap shots* and *hitting below the belt*. It painted a picture - though, admittedly, not exactly a pretty picture. But it made people want to read further.

Anyway, the headline can make or break your direct mail letter - so devote a ton of time coming up with a good one. Don't settle for the first headline that comes into your mind.

In fact, the title of this book probably went through at least two dozen changes, alternations and refinements even after I settled on the subject line.

So take out a legal pad and write down dozens - even hundreds - of possible headlines. And if you want to really study the art of great headline writing, go to the grocery store and - now don't laugh - scan copies of the National Enquirer, the Globe, the Star, etc.

These so-called tabloid magazines employ some of the best headline writers in the business.

Every headline on the front page is written in a way that piques your curiosity and draws you into the body of the magazine. Every headline above a story is written to draw you into the body copy. And the first paragraph is written in slightly larger text to help lead you into the second paragraph. And so on…

Cosmopolitan magazine is also great at headline writing. Again, the bottom line is: Imitate success. Don't reinvent the wheel.

Some additional tips:

1. The safest headline begins with the words, *"How to…"*
2. Headline should generally be no longer than 17 words in length. Instead of a longer headline, use a sub-headline.
3. Placing quotation marks around the headline makes it more memorable and powerful.
4. Don't use reverse type. It's harder to read.
5. Always use upper and lower case letters. USING ALL CAPITAL LETTERS MAKES YOUR TEXT HARDER TO READ.
6. Don't vary the type size or style - no matter how avant-garde you think your readers are.
7. Use verbs that are strong and colorful, such as *slash, betray, punish,* or *cheat.*
8. Use the present tense, not the future tense. It gives your message a sense of immediacy.
9. Use short words.

10. Never put a period at the end of a headline. This gives the reader an opportunity to stop. You want him to keep on going. Question marks and exclamation points are OK, though.

11. The two most powerful headline words you can use are *you* and *free*.

Other words or phrases which work extremely well in a headline include, *new, now, announcing, the truth about, protect, here, life, amazing, yes, discover, do you, love, how much*, and *only*.

Again, your headline can make or break your direct mail letter, so you should spend as much as 80 percent of your time just coming up with a real blockbuster.

## SECRET #7: BENEFITS VS. FEATURES

Soliciting someone for a contribution is no different from asking someone to join a record-and-tape club. People buy with their hearts, not with their heads. You must stir feelings if you're going to get someone to dust the cobwebs off their wallet and part with their hard-earned cash. So you need to provide an emotional appeal as well as a rational appeal.

That means giving the reader both the features of your offer...and the benefits.

To understand this better, break out some of those letters in your *swipe* file. As you read them, you'll come across certain claims being made by the writer, such as *"our organization has 2 million members, a spiffy new logo and brand new offices in Podunk."*

These are features - to which the reader's response is often, *"So what? What's that mean to me?"* WIFM again.

If you really want to pull in the big bucks, you need to load up your direct mail letter with benefits that actually benefit the reader - not the writer. It's actually easier than it sounds. All you do is complete the following sentence: *"You get..."*

If the sentence in your letter is an *"I (we) have..."* - that's a feature. If the sentence says, *"You get..."* - that's a benefit. Load your letter up with *"You gets."*

One final note: People are much more motivated by a fear of loss than they are by the hope of gain. Scaring the dickens out of your audience is a sure-fire way to stir up their emotions...and loosen the purse strings.

*"If you don't help us, our opponents will steal your retirement benefits!"*

Scary...and powerful. On the other hand:

*"If you help us, we'll work to raise your retirement benefits to keep up with the cost of living."*

Good...but not quite as compelling.

## SECRET #8: LENGTH

One of the most often-asked questions I get at fundraising direct mail training seminars is, *"How long should the letter be?"*

Good question. It reminds me of a question Abe Lincoln was reportedly once asked: *"How long should a man's legs be?"* To which the president replied, *"Long enough to reach the floor."*

The same is true for direct mail.

Your letter should be as long as it takes to get the job done. If you can tell your story and persuade someone to send you money with one page, that's how long the letter should be. If it takes you, two, four, eight or even 16 pages - that's how long it should be.

But think about this.

Most people don't meet for the first time and get married the same day. You naturally want to know a lot about an individual before making such a strong commitment.

The same is true when it comes to getting people to donate money to you - especially for the first time. They need to know as much as possible before making such a strong commitment - and spending their money is certainly a strong commitment.

To put it another way: *"The more you tell, the more you sell."*

If your reader isn't familiar with you, your organization or what it is you do, you'd better devote considerable time to revealing every bit of pertinent information you can think of - features and benefits. Nobody wants to buy a pig in a poke. They want details, details, details...

Now...as a general rule, a two-page letter will outdraw a one-page letter; a four-page letter will outdraw a two-page letter; an eight-page letter will outdraw a four-page letter, etc.

The bottom line: A direct mail letter can't be too long...but it can be too boring. Don't throw crud into your letter just to make it longer. Every word must have relevance - and that means relevance to the reader, not the writer.

One final word of caution on this subject: Some of your best friends and closest advisers will tell you that no one will read a long letter and advise you to keep it short. They're just plain WRONG! Ignore them...for they know not what they speak.

The more you tell, the more you sell. The more you tell, the more you sell. The more you tell...

## SECRET #9: BODY COPY

As I mentioned earlier, writing isn't exactly brain surgery...but some people have more of a talent for it than others. If you can afford to hire a professional copywriter, the money will likely be well spent. If not, here are a few suggestions which will help.

Write like you talk. You're writing what is supposed to be a personal letter - no matter how many thousands of people you're mailing the same letter to. This is not a term paper. It should read like a letter from your best friend. The tone should be friendly, warm and sincere. Don't shout or scream in your text.

Use short words, short sentences and short paragraphs. A paragraph should normally be no more than four or five lines. One sentence paragraphs are a good way to break up the text. Use one word sentences occasionally, also.

Personalize your salutation if at all possible. *"Dear Mr. Jones,"* is much better than *"Dear Fellow Republican."* If you can't personalize the salutation, your best opening is, *"Dear Friend."*

Make sure your first sentence has power - almost as much power as your headline. The first sentence should force the reader into the second sentence, and so forth, throughout the letter.

Here are 15 examples of great opening lines, courtesy of *Direct Marketing Magazine*...

> *"If you're like me..."*
> *"I (we) need your help..."*
> *"As you know..."*
> *"We don't know each other, but it's time we did."*
> *"This is disgusting, and you're the one to fix it..."*

*"I've got bad news and I've got good news..."*
*"Did you know..."*
*"You and I are in trouble and here's what you'd better do..."*
*"Believe it or not..."*
*"Ouch!"*
*"When was the last time you..."*
*"These are critical times..."*
*"I'll get right to the point..."*
*"In the time it took you to open this envelope..."*
*"Are you really sure they're giving you the right facts..."*

Once again, some well-meaning friends and associates may tell you that you should save your best stuff for last. Once again, don't listen to them. Always start off strong. If you don't, the odds are your reader will toss your letter long before he gets to your *best stuff.*

Avoid using the word *"I."* It's the biggest turnoff in copywriting. Instead, reword every sentence possible using the words *you* or *your.* That's the way to write reader-centered copy.

When you finish the first rough-draft of your direct mail letter, take your red pen and circle the words *I* and *me* wherever you find them. Then go back and try to change them to *you* or *your.*

Also, eliminate the word *"that"* wherever possible. It's the most overused word in any direct mail letter.

Finally, and with all due respect to your elementary school English teacher, throw the grammar book out the window.

Remember, write like you talk. Go ahead and end a sentence with a preposition if you want to. It won't hurt (I just did it.). Go ahead and start a sentence with *and* or *but.* And an occasional use of *ain't* ain't bad, either. It makes you sound more...human. Just like your reader.

It's also a good idea to occasionally use some familiar old sayings to give your writing that personal, down-home feel. Such as, *"That dog won't hunt"* or *"Up a creek without a paddle."* This is the sort of thing that will get people to like you - and people give money to people they like.

## SECRET #10: FORMAT

Here are some additional *mechanical* tips:

- For ease of reading - and cost - use white paper.
- Off-white, pale yellow, blue, green or pink can also be used...but avoid *astrobright* colors. You want your letter to appear personal.
- The paper weight should be at least 20-lbs. The paper should *feel* substantial, not flimsy.
- Always use a serif typeface in the body copy. (Serif fonts have the little *feet* attached to each letter, such as the fonts in this book). Sans serif (like this) is harder to read.
- A Courier-style font is often better than a Times Roman font. The typewritten look out-pulls the typeset look...but this may be changing as more and more people enter the computer world.
- A twelve-point font is standard - anything smaller is often difficult for elderly people to read.
- The text should always be printed in black - and darker type increases response.
- Use sub-heads (mini-headlines) to break up large blocks of copy.
- Use bullets (·) to break up copy and add emphasis (as we're doing right now).
- Also, underline words for emphasis...but don't go nuts. Only underline <u>key</u> words.
- Your margins should be at least 3/4"-to-1" all the way around.
- Don't end a page with the end of a sentence. Force the reader to turn to the next page to complete the sentence.
- Include the words, *"Please continue to next page..."* at the end of each page.

This stuff may sound trivial, but it's often the difference between making money and losing money on a direct mail project.

## SECRET #11: THE CLOSE

Getting contributions through direct mail is just like any other sales transaction - you must ask for the money! More than once. And don't leave the amount up to the donor. Ask for a specific amount.

If your letter says, *"Please send us whatever you feel appropriate,"* you've placed a tremendous and unwarranted burden on your donor. The donor won't want to send too little (he doesn't want you to think he's a cheapskate). But he won't want to send too much, either (then you might think he's a chump).

So rather than risk being perceived as either cheap or a chump, the donor more than likely will just not respond at all. That's not what you want.

Now, obviously, different people have different financial abilities to contribute. So give everyone a choice.

Include a low number (which represents the smallest contribution you'd like to receive), an intermediate number (which represents the amount you really hope most people will send), and a high number (which represents an amount you'd be thrilled to get). You also want to include *Other* along with a space for the donor to write in an amount *other* than the selections you've presented him or her.

So...your appeal might sound something like this:

> *"Please send your most generous contribution of $100, $50, $25 or whatever you think appropriate."*

Always start with your highest request and work your way down. This is just basic salesmanship.

How many car salesmen do you know who start at the dealer's *cost* and then try to get you to pay more? None. They start high and come down...slowly.

Make sure you create a sense of urgency in your request. Action delayed is action not taken. A person who sets your letter aside probably won't come back to it. You need to persuade your potential contributor to open up the checkbook now! Not tomorrow. NOW!

Throwing in a *bonus* is a great way to get immediate action. Something such as:

> *"The first 100 people to send in a contribution of $25 or more will receive a FREE autographed photo of Senator Funderpuck."*

Or...

> *"Everyone who sends a contribution by October 7th will receive FREE VIP seating at the annual Christmas dinner."*

Nothing motivates people more than the prospect of getting something for nothing - so long as the something is something of real value.

Finally, the signature must always be in *process blue* ink. Not black...not red...not green. Blue.

And only have one person sign the letter. Not two...not three. One. A personal letter is sent from one individual to another individual (sometimes a couple, such as husband and wife). Having more than one signer on your letter defeats the purpose of making it a personal appeal.

## SECRET #12: THE POSTSCRIPT

Every letter MUST include a good P.S.

As I mentioned earlier, the P.S. is one of the first things people look at after opening your envelope - not the last. That's why it's important to devote considerable time and attention to what you say in the P.S.

Use this opportunity to summarize your request and ask again for the donation. Remind people why it's important to act TODAY. And don't be afraid to use the P.S. to introduce a surprise bonus for the contributor. The P.S. is one of the most important selling opportunities in a direct mail letter. Don't waste it.

## SECRET #13: THE ORDER FORM

Many people will open your envelope and look at the order form first...before reading the letter itself. Therefore, it's to your benefit to also devote considerable time to the design and wording of the reply card.

Give the response devise as much attention as you give the letter. Some suggestions...

- *Repeat your headline*
- *Use an attractive border*
- *Use an appealing title, such as "Charter Subscription Offer," "Limited Edition Certificate," "Special Application," or "Reservation Request"*
- *Print in at least two colors*
- *Print on different paper stock from the letter*

## SECRET #14: THE RETURN ENVELOPE

You must...MUST...include a self-addressed return envelope in your direct mail package. Tests have shown that just the inclusion of an envelope boosts response by 33 percent. You want to make it as easy as possible for the donor to actually send in his contribution. If he has to look for an envelope, he may well lose interest. Don't take that chance. Supply him with an envelope.

Should you also pay for the return postage?

There are different opinions on this. Some professionals say the donor will have no problem paying the postage. They may have a point - and this will definitely save you a few pennies. But remember the old saying about being penny wise and a pound foolish. Not providing the return postage can even make you look *cheap*.

I come down on the side of the very basics: Make it as easy for the donor to give as is humanly possible. Why risk a possible $25 donation over the cost of a stamp?

On a cost/benefit basis, I say pay for the postage. But go to the post office, pay to get a pre-paid postal permit. That way, you only pay postage for the envelopes which are actually sent back to you. (The amount you pay is slightly higher than first-class postage, but it's still a bargain). If you want to save a few pennies, include a little note on the return envelope that says something like: *"Your stamp on this envelope will help save us much-needed funds."*

## SECRET #15: LIFT LETTERS

A lift letter (or *pub note*) is called a lift letter because it's purpose is to *lift* response.

If you're an unknown candidate running for a state legislative seat - and you want to make a direct appeal under your own signature for contributions - try to get someone with higher name recognition or community standing to sign a separate note to be included in your package.

The lift letter should have a different tone from the main letter and be printed on a different-colored paper stock. It should be, or include, a testimonial. For example:

> *"Hello, I'm Governor Muth and I've known Joe Sixpack for 17 years. He's the kind of representative we need in government and I urge you to generously support his campaign."*

Of course, you can embellish and lengthen the lift letter more than I have here, but you get the idea. Still, your lift letter should be brief - no more than one page long. Keep it to about 150 words or less.

## SECRET #16: GRABBERS

*Grabbers* are a staple of the direct mail industry. They are used to *grab* your attention - thus the name. The most successful grabber in political direct mail fundraising is the *membership card*. Year in and year out, membership card mailings continue to outperform all others.

Here are some examples of other *grabbers:*

- *Opinion surveys (but be careful not to insult the intelligence of your donors by asking brain-dead questions, such as: "Do you support lower taxes?" Duh.)*
- *Certificates of Appreciation*
- *Newsletters*
- *Photos*
- *Calendars*

## SECRET #17: THANK YOU'S

This is the single most important way to ensure that once a contributor gives to you once, he'll give to you again and again and again...

And it's the most overlooked as well.

Not only is saying *"thank you"* good manners and a common courtesy - things woefully lacking in our society today - but it's good business as well. If your contributor doesn't believe you genuinely appreciate his or her generosity, they'll eventually feel taken advantage of.

No one wants to be a sucker.

And because so few people take the time to say *"thank you,"* your note of appreciation will be recognized and valued all the more.

Here again, your well-meaning friends and associates might try to tell you that people don't expect a thank you when giving to a charitable cause or campaign; that they'll appreciate the fact that you haven't wasted their money on a stamp and a thank you card or letter.

And once again, you tell your well-meaning friend or associate to stick a sock in it.

Nothing...and I mean NOTHING...is as important as saying thank you to someone who generously took money out of his or her pocket and put it in yours. If you've neglected to perform this common courtesy in the past, go to the chalk board, right now, and write, *"Always Say Thank You!"* one hundred times.

That's it. Direct mail is a process and a skill you never stop learning - but hopefully this information will give you a bit of an advantage over your competition.

Live long and prosper.

# WANT TO LEARN EVEN MORE ABOUT FUNDRAISING?

## The Secrets to Raising a Boatload of Money for Your Campaign or Organization...Especially if You <u>HATE</u> Fundraising!

If you're not raising the amount of money your campaign needs to win your race, there is one person and only one person to blame.

Look in the mirror. However...

*Unless you have an extensive background in sales, it's not your fault. It is, however, your responsibility to fix.*

Fortunately, I can help you. Man, oh, man, can I help you! Because I've been in your shoes. Ran for office in 1996. Hated fundraising. Didn't raise the money I needed. *Got creamed on Election Day.*

Then things changed. And over the past 10 years, I've raised well over $5 million for what has mostly been a one-person non-profit organization primarily operating in a very small population state - Nevada.

How did I do it? What changed? More importantly, can you do it to?

Absolutely. And that brings me to… *The #1 secret to raising a boatload of money for your campaign.*

WWE professional wrestler John Cena has a signature move called the "AA" – which stands for *Attitude Adjustment.*

And if you want to raise more money for your campaign (or non-profit organization, or even your own business), that's probably exactly what you need. An attitude adjustment.

Here's a *one-question test* to see if your campaign's fundraising problem is your attitude. Now answer it honestly…

> *Have you ever considered doing something in your campaign*
> *but said, "We can't afford to do that"?*

If the answer to that question is *yes*, you have an attitude problem. The good news, however, is that it's a problem you can fix very simply, very easily and very quickly.

STEP ONE: Never say *"We can't afford to do that"* again. Instead say, *"We can't afford NOT to do that, so how do we raise the money?"*

You see, as Dan Sullivan of Strategic Coach is fond of saying, *"The problem isn't the problem; the problem is how you think about the problem."*

I swear, if you just make this one little attitude adjustment in your campaign – no longer saying *"we can't afford to do that"* - you're going to see your fundraising skyrocket!

Of course, like many things in life, that's easier said than done. But since I'm the Campaign Doctor, let me give you *three prescriptions* to help heal your case of *Stinkin' Thinkin'*.

## 1. Stop Making the "Bad Economy" Excuse.

Have you ever heard the sports term *loser's limp*? The Urban Dictionary defines *loser's limp* thusly:

> *"An ailment or impediment that is feigned or exaggerated by a competitor to explain a poor performance."*

Is the economy bad right now? Of course. Obama's still president. Duh.

And yet...

In 2008, AT THE HEIGHT OF THE GREAT RECESSION, Bloomberg reported that *"Campaign spending was more than double that of four years ago."*

Double! Right smack dab in the middle of the housing meltdown and financial disaster.

"The 2008 campaign was the costliest in history," Politico reported, "with a record-shattering $5.3 billion in spending by candidates, political parties and interest groups on the congressional and presidential races."

Fast-forward to the 2012 election cycle. Campaign spending shattered that 2008 record, with combined spending exceeding a staggering $6 billion. And in that election, President Obama alone *attracted over 4 million small dollar donors!*

So don't for one minute think there's no money out there for your campaign because of the bad economy. That's just an excuse. A loser's limp. If you're blaming the bad economy for your lack of fundraising success, adjust your attitude…right now. Because it is NOT the economy's fault.

## 2. Money isn't given; it's raised.

If you think people wake up in the morning and say to themselves, "You know, I really want to give some of my money to a political candidate today," you are sadly mistaken. Fundraising just doesn't work that way.

*The #1 reason why a person doesn't give to a political campaign is simple…*

They weren't asked.

Now if the thought of asking complete strangers for money for your campaign is more horrifying than the thought of waking up in a bed full of black widow spiders, then you need to do one of three things…

   *(a) Self-fund your campaign*
   *(b) Drop out of the race*
   *(c) Overcome your fear of asking for money*

I'm going to assume that if you're reading this book, (a) is not an option. And considering how much better off we all would be if you were elected, I hope (b) is not an option. Which leave us with (c). *And I can help you there with one very simple, totally painless exercise.*

Unless you are a salesman by profession, asking for money from strangers is probably an alien and uncomfortable act. If that's the case, then your problem isn't *raising* money; it's *asking* for money. So here's what you do…

Every person you meet on the campaign trail – EVERY ONE – at the end of the conversation you ask them for ONE DOLLAR.

That's it. $1.

Will that dollar make a dent in the campaign budget you need to raise? Hardly. But that's not the point. The point is to get you over your fear and discomfort of asking for money.

As Fred DeLuca, the founder of Subway, famously and wisely advised: *"Make pennies first."*

His point, as psychologist Maxwell Maltz explained, is that "it is easier to envision making dollars if you've made pennies, easier to envision making thousands if you've made hundreds." Bingo!

And if it helps, just blame me. Say something like this…

> *"Mr. Johnson, thanks for taking time to speak with me about the city council race. But to be perfectly honest, I'm really, really uncomfortable asking people for money. And I have this crazy consultant who is making me ask every person I talk to if they'd consider donating just one dollar to our campaign to help me overcome my fear of fundraising. Would you be able to spare a dollar to help us out?"*

This way it's not *you* asking for the dollar; it's me *making* you ask for the dollar. And if you can't even do that, then maybe you better seriously consider option (b) above.

*Now here's the good news: This works!*

A candidate I coached in a recent Republican primary had the exact same paralyzing fear of fundraising you might be having right now. It was truly a pain for her to even ask for $1. But she started doing it.

*And people started giving her money.*

Not enough to fund her campaign. But enough to give her the confidence and comfort to start asking for higher and higher amounts. And I can't tell you how excited she was when she called to tell me she'd just gotten her first $500 contribution!

Another candidate I coached in a different race took the "$1 ask" to heart and asked every single person she came across while walking door-to-door for a buck. And she told me she raised over $500 alone from that habit in the 12 weeks of her primary race.

*Oh, and here's an extraordinary side benefit to the "$1 ask"…*

Everyone who gives you even just one dollar is now financially invested in your campaign. In most cases, *even a pack of pit bulls couldn't make them vote for your opponent.*

## 3. You are what you think.

Now I don't want to get all existential on you here – especially since I'm not really sure what existential even means – but here's a powerful and important piece of advice from Buddha…

> *"We are what we think. All that we are arises with our thoughts."*

Now bear with me here, because this is a critical concept to embed in your campaign.

If you spend all day thinking about issues – how to fix education, how to fix government over-spending, how to fix health care, how to fix immigration – at the end of the day you're going to have a lot of ideas about a lot of issues. But what you won't have is…

*The money you need to get elected to fix those problems!*

First things first.

If your immediate campaign problem is fundraising, not issue development, then you need to adjust what you think about most of the time during the day. You need to spend most of your time re-adjusting your thinking to raising money, raising money and raising money.

You should wake up in the morning thinking about raising money, think about raising money throughout the day, and go to bed thinking about raising money.

Because if you don't have the money you need to do the things you need to win, nothing else really matters. Are you with me?

Now I'm assuming if you're still reading this far into this book, maybe fundraising isn't exactly a subject you know a lot about. Don't let that stop you. You're in luck!

A LOT of people have been in your shoes. And a LOT of people are in your shoes right now.

Fortunately, there is an abundance of books, CDs, videos, podcasts, newsletters, courses, workshops and trainers to help you become not just competent in fundraising, but an outright expert.

*Indeed, like great salesmen, great fundraisers aren't born. They're made.*

In his book *The Ultimate Success Secret*, author and marketing legend Dan Kennedy lists *"The 7 Ways to Get Smarter about Virtually any Subject – FAST."*

1. Find and read at least a year's back issues of related trade or specialty magazines
2. Answer a lot of the ads you find in these magazines
3. Find the top experts, most successful people, and most celebrated people in the field
4. Find the books written by "the OLD masters"
5. Join trade associations or clubs
6. Take a class, workshop or seminar
7. Do your homework

So if you need money for your campaign but don't know how to raise money for your campaign, you not only need to start learning the basics of fundraising, but *you need to commit yourself* to a never-ending quest to learn more and more and more about fundraising.

In academia it's called *continuing education*. And if you don't know where to start, I have the perfect prescription for you…

### www.FastStartFundraising.com

Don't worry, it's free. And there you'll find *"How to Raise Your First $5,000…and a Whole Lot More."*

The late, great marketing guru Gary Halbert was fond of saying, *"Motion beats meditation."* And he was so right.

Yes, you need to start thinking about fundraising and thinking about fundraising and then thinking some more about fundraising…to the point where almost your entire campaign existence is dominated by the thought of raising money.

> *But be warned: Unless you actually put those thoughts to deeds, it won't mean squat.*

On the other hand, if you get dead serious about execution and implementation, there is nothing that can stop you from raising 10, 20 or even 100 times what you currently *think* you can raise.

As Henry Ford said, *"Whether you think you can, or you think you can't-- you're right."*

I don't just think you can. I KNOW you can. The question, however, is: What do YOU think?

And remember, from this day forward, never again say, *"We can't afford to do that."* Instead, always say, *"We can't afford NOT to do that, so how do we raise the money?"*

And the first step towards answering that question is to go to **www.FastStartFundraising.com** right NOW!

# ABOUT THE AUTHOR

Chuck Muth is the founder of *The Campaign Doctor* and president of *Desert Fox Strategic Communications*, a political and government affairs consulting firm.

He is also president of *Citizen Outreach*, a conservative non-profit organization, a former executive director of the *American Conservative Union*, and a former national chairman of the *Republican Liberty Caucus*.

Chuck is an author, Nevada's leading conservative blogger, an independent self-syndicated columnist, and a regular guest on political and public affairs TV and radio programs.

He and his wife Gia, their two daughters, Kristen and Jenna, son CJ, and a menagerie of critters and pets that could fill up an Ark all live in Las Vegas, Nevada.

For more information go to www.ChuckMuth.com

www.ingramcontent.com/pod-product-compliance
Lightning Source LLC
Chambersburg PA
CBHW021431170526
45164CB00001B/188